HOTEL
SCARBADOS

Mark Harland.

HOTEL SCARBADOS

A novel set in Yorkshire
in the third decade of the 21st century

MARK HARLAND

Published by MVH Publishing 2024

A CIP catalogue record for this book is available from the British Library.

ISBN 978-1-7397547-3-0 (Paperback)
ISBN 978-1-7397547-4-7 (ePub)

Book layout by Clare Brayshaw

Prepared and printed by:

York Publishing Services Ltd
64 Hallfield Road
Layerthorpe
York
YO31 7ZQ

Tel: 01904 431213

Website: www.yps-publishing.co.uk

AUTHOR'S NOTE

Several years ago BBC Television broadcast a six-part comedy series called simply – 'SCARBOROUGH.' It was beautifully filmed and was great publicity for the town. Sadly, and inexplicably, it was not repeated and the first series was also the last. It left millions of viewers wanting more!

I wrote to the BBC to complain and urged them to rename the programme 'SCARBADOS' and to start again with new scriptwriters. My letter was read out word for word on BBC Radio York – to no avail.

I hope this book, and possibly its sequels, will go some way to compensate all those disappointed viewers. If you haven't been to 'Scarbados' then I urge you to come and visit.

This is a novel and all characters are fictitious. Any clash with real people is purely co-incidental.

I would like to offer my sincere thanks to the superb team of people at York Publishing Services (YPS) and to my dear friend, Barbara Ralph, who patiently guided me through the plot over several months.

Mark Harland

1.

The redundancy notice from P & O Ferries hit Peter Fishburn hard. He'd worked on the MV Pride of Bruges as a Senior Steward for almost twenty years. The notice, which was sent Recorded Delivery to his home address in Hull, had arrived a week ago but after opening it he had secreted it in his work travel bag. He eventually summoned up the courage to show it to his wife of almost twenty years. There were tears and hugs from wife Mandy and the three kids, two girls and a boy, all in their late teens. At fifty-seven he was too young to retire, even if he wanted to, which he didn't. And most employers would consider him too old, despite new anti-ageism laws.

'Something'll crop up Dad' said his auburn haired eldest and his unofficial favourite. At twenty Millie was studying Business and Accountancy and working part-time in a motel not far from the ferry terminal.

Mandy was deeply upset but tried not to show it in front of Pete and the kids. When Peter reported for duty on his next trip to Belgium she wasted no time in calling an old friend, Margaret, a workmate from when they both worked together at Marks & Sparks in Whitefriargate. They met for coffee in a café opposite Hull Paragon train station.

'Oh Margaret, I just don't know what we're going to do. In a month's time there'll be no money coming in. I'll have to look for a job. At least Jamie and Lucy are a bit older now. It's not just us is it? Lots of families in Hull will be affected.'

'Those redundancies had been predicted in the local press for a long time. I know that doesn't help, love, but try to stay positive.'

And then fate intervened. Two weeks after the redundancy notice a heavy white envelope arrived in the post addressed to Mrs Amanda Fishburn. The franking mark revealed that its origin was the local firm of solicitors Hymer & Hymer of Silver Street, Hull. What on earth could this be? Taking a small knife from the plastic-handled set on the kitchen worktop, Mandy slit it open. At least six pages were enclosed, the top one a formal letter:

Dear Mrs Fishburn

In the matter of the late Mary Mildred Leonard

We act as Executors for the above named deceased who died in Preston in the District of Holderness on 1st December last year. We must apologise for the delay in contacting you which has, in part at least, been caused by the Covid pandemic.

As you can see from the attached copy of the late Mrs Leonard's Will, you are listed as one of several beneficiaries. There are a number of modest legacies to animal charities which take priority in the distribution of assets. We have gone to great lengths to trace the other beneficiary apart from your good self, a Mr Douglas Leonard, and a stepson of the deceased. It would seem that he died many years ago in a mining accident in Sudbury, Ontario, was unmarried without progeny and thus you are the sole beneficiary. We attach a copy of the Will and a provisional Statement of Assets. The latter is not yet complete as we are waiting for valuations from Barclays Bank where various documents were held for safe-keeping. The branch of the bank in question was in Trinity House Lane which closed and merged with another branch many years ago. Documents were transferred to a central storage unit elsewhere in the country and the Schedule is, thus far, only provisional.

You will see from the Schedule that there are several foreign securities listed including shares in Canadian and Australian companies. You will recall that your aunt's late husband, Martin Leonard, predeceased her by over ten years and little, if any, attention has appeared to have been paid to those holdings. Mr Leonard had worked as a geologist in both those countries long before he met and married your aunt and it is quite possible that she knew little or nothing about them. We have been able to value the listed Australian mining companies as they are listed on the Sydney Stock Exchange but take note these valuations are current and not at the date of your aunt's death which will be the relevant date for Probate purposes. The Canadian mining shares have been similarly provisionally valued but you must also bear in mind they are valued in dollars, as are the Australian holdings. The holdings in the Hudson Bay Trading Company are posing the biggest problem as they are 'bearer shares' and although the nominal number of shares held is listed as five thousand, until we receive the certificate itself a true valuation cannot even be guessed. As a precaution it has a nil valuation thus far.

In summary, and taking into account an approximate and amateur valuation for Skylark Cottage in the village of Preston as two hundred and fifty thousand pounds, the provisional total value of the estate is between four and five hundred thousand pounds.

With the lock-down rules coming into force seemingly with every day that passes, it is regretted that it might be some weeks before matters can even begin to be formalised but we have written to Barclays and asked for the Hudson Bay Trading Company certificate to be sent to us as a matter of urgency. We must advise you that obtaining Probate and thus being able to distribute funds in accordance with Mrs Leonard's Will could take many months, indeed possibly until the end of this year.

I would be happy to discuss any of the aforementioned matters with you, of course, but must tell you that our offices will be closed from this Friday for the Easter holiday until the following Wednesday. After that, telephone or zoom meetings will replace appointments in our office until Government restrictions have been scaled-down.

Yours faithfully

Hymer & Hymer Solicitors.

Mandy, read the letter two more times. It was hard to take in. Her Aunt Mary had been very much a recluse and had discouraged visitors for years. She had been Millie's godmother but the only regular contact had been a perfunctory birthday card every year with a twenty pound note and a 'buy yourself something nice' message enclosed. Pete was upstairs and packing his case to prepare himself for the last trip he would make to Belgium, as a crew member anyway. It was only three in the afternoon and they would

4

normally share tea and biscuits together before Mandy would drive Pete down to King George docks. Had the letter not arrived then this last drive to work would have the air of a funeral cortege.

'Pete, sit down love and read this while I put the kettle on.'

To say that they were both in shock was a gross understatement.

'When shall we tell the kids? Should we tell them anything yet, Pete?'

'Of course we should. In their own way they're as worried as us about my future job prospects. Drink up and drive me down to the Dock. I don't want to be late for my last trip, now do I?'

An hour later and Pete Fishburn, Senior Steward, was on Red Deck checking the Food & Beverage manifest prior to sailing in two hours time. The ferry was packed with passengers as rumours abounded that this would be the last 'Mini-cruise' to Belgium before travel restrictions on the Continent forced the closure of the whole route. The good folks of Hull and East Yorkshire didn't want to go short of duty-free tobacco and booze for a lock-down of unknown duration. Now did they?

It was a busy night in the Sunset Bar on the Pride of Bruges but in between serving customers he couldn't take his mind off that solicitor's letter that had arrived out of the blue. Let's assume the low valuation of four hundred grand, mused Pete to himself. At even two percent per annum interest rate that's eight grand a year or about a hundred and sixty quid a week and you still had the capital. Certainly the future looked a lot brighter than it had done a few hours earlier. Then there was the redundancy money from P & O to add to that about which he was still awaiting final details.

'You look happy Pete considering you're about to be unemployed' a fellow Steward remarked to him.

'Always look on the bright side of life' replied Pete in a quip from the Python movie The Life of Brian.'

Naturally he didn't mention the windfall that was going to change his and his family's life forever. But if he could have been a fly on the wall back at Noseley Way in Kingswood, East Hull the conversation would not have been about interest rates or weekly income.

2.

With Millie back home from her evening class and the two 'youngsters' Jamie seventeen, and Lucy almost sixteen, all four of them were in the living room waiting for an episode of their favourite detective series, 'Vera', to commence. There would soon be a ring at the doorbell to announce the arrival of a pizza delivery man on a moped from the parlour not too far away. That was their Thursday night routine but Dad's redundancy notice and loss of earnings would soon put the kibosh on such extravagances.

The pizzas, a Hawaiian and a Margherita duly arrived which were immediately rushed into the kitchen to be sliced up by Jamie wielding the professional looking circular saw. Lucy was busy making a cafétiere of Java coffee, her and her mother's favourite. It was two minutes to eight o'clock, the starting time for Vera. They just made it and plonked themselves down onto the two twin sofas, much to the consternation of Seb, the family's labradoodle, who was relegated to the rug. The opening music and credits started and to everyone else's shock horror the matriarch of the family reached for the TV remote control and switched the set off. Lucy reacted first.

'Mam! What are doing? Mam!'

Such was her knee jerk physical reaction that a chunk of sun-dried tomato slid off her slice of pizza down her chin and onto her favourite cream coloured Tommy Hillfiger top.

'Now look what you've made me do!'

She ran into the kitchen for a cloth and returned seconds later with that annoyed Viking look on her face. She was even more annoyed when she saw that her mother was half laughing at her. Mandy took control.

'We can all watch Vera later on Catchup. I have something to read to you all.'

Mandy read the solicitor's letter to them word for word, pausing several times between paragraphs for a slurp of Java. Silence ruled for about ten seconds whilst the kids took it all in. Millie reacted first.

'Does Dad know? Why have you waited until he was back at sea? He'll be way down the Humber estuary now. Let's call him! He might still just be able to get a signal on his mobile. They have access to that North Sea cellphone link don't they? I know they do because I've spoken to him at sea – sometimes in the middle of the night if I was awake.'

This came as no surprise to Mandy who knew that the bond between Millie and her father was very close.

'Your Dad knows everything. We agreed before he sailed that I would tell you everything this evening. I want us to have a full discussion about our family's future over the next few days before the Pride of Bruges returns to Hull which marks the end of your Dad's seafaring career.'

The pizza slices were cooling down and taken to the microwave for thirty seconds nuking. More coffee was made and tins of Diet Coke retrieved from the fridge. And then the cacophony commenced.

'Let's open a pet shop with the money' barked Lucy who was closer to Seb emotionally than the rest of the family.

'I say let's open a fish & chip shop' suggested Jamie. The nearest one's a mile from here! I could do home deliveries once I pass my motorbike test. It's a winner!'

'What about you, Millie? What do you suggest?'

'I say let's leave Hull, move up the coast and buy a B & B guest house or a small hotel.'

More silence, followed by shock horror from the rest.

'You've been watching too much of that Hotel Inspector programme and that other one – Four in the Bed. We wouldn't last five minutes. Covid has stuffed the tourist and hospitality industries. Millie reacted quickly.

'That's the whole point. Many existing businesses will be in trouble, particularly those with a high asset to borrowing ratio.' Her evening classes were coming in useful already although she had heard today that henceforth they would all be online and via zoom because of the Covid restrictions. It therefore didn't matter to her where she lived, she would still complete the remaining eighteen months of her course and earn the Diploma. She had the floor and continued, feeling almost in charge. She was too but didn't realise just how persuasive she was until many months later.

'Look, just out of interest, lets look on Rightmove and Zoopla and checkout small hotels in Hornsea and Bridlington being as they're the nearest to us. We've nothing to lose have we? It'll be fun as well. I'll go and get my laptop that I bought to help me with my course.'

Talk about excitement! Even dear Vera had been forgotten. It was eleven o'clock by the time they all turned in for bed to dream about a B&B overlooking Hornsea Mere or a small hotel in sight of the stunning white cliffs of Flamborough Head.

On the North Sea the Pride of Bruges was heading south east and was approaching the half-way point of the two hundred nautical mile sector to Zeebrugge. The on-board entertainers, a male keyboards player and a female singer, were coming to the end of their third and final session.

Within an hour Pete would be in his cabin and sleeping only fitfully. The interest on four hundred grand wouldn't even cover half of his current earnings. If he'd been privy to the family chatter a hundred miles behind him he would have had a dicky-fit. By nature he wasn't a risk-taker and when the money came in as far as he was concerned it was going to be the Yorkshire Penny Bank (as he still called it) or the Post Office. Eventually he fell asleep and dreamt about whiling hours away in a futile search of jobs vacancies in the Hull Daily Mail.

At eight o'clock the following morning the Pride of Bruges nudged slowly alongside the Leopold Terminal and tied up. Pete decided to spend the day in Bruges and grabbed a seat on the complimentary coach service into the City itself. After all, he might not get the chance again for a long time, if ever. What a depressing thought.

Back in Hull it was all go! Sandwiches were made, flasks of coffee prepared and Seb's biscuits and water bowl stored in the back of the family car, a modest five year old estate. Next stop the coast. This was going to be an adventure!

3.

The A165 was extremely quiet. More Covid rules were coming into force. They were only a couple of miles short of Hornsea when the already thin traffic started to slow down, almost to crawling speed. Mandy was driving although Millie had passed her Test several months earlier.

"I can see two police cars about a hundred yards up front, one on each side of the road. Don't tell me there's been an accident and the road's blocked.'

Within a few seconds of coming to a complete halt a uniformed officer of Humberside Police tapped on the drivers' window and indicated for the window to be wound down. He was polite but firm.

'Is this journey completely essential, Madam?' Mandy was not impressed but kept her cool.

'I beg your pardon, officer. What on earth are you implying? We don't live in a Police state yet, or do we?'

'Madam, did you hear the Prime Minister on radio and television last night? New travel restrictions are coming into force with immediate effect. All non-essential travel is prohibited. Where exactly are you going and why?' Mandy started to lose it, as Viking descendants are apt to do.

'If you must bloody know, officer, we're off to Brid to see a man about a dog. Seb in the back here is responding to a dog-dating chat-line and ...' The officer was not amused.

'Can I see your driving licence please madam? Mandy reached into her purse and produced the pink plastic licence for the officer to examine.

'I'm sorry madam but I must ask you to return to your home address in Kingswood HU7 without delay'

He was interrupted by his walkie-talkie squawking at him like a parrot with dysentery. It was a colleague from the other Police car who seemed to be having a serious altercation with the driver of a white Transit van who was wanting to drive south towards Hull. Everybody could hear him.

'Now look 'ere Officer, I'm 'alfway through doing a roofing job for an old lady in Orchard Park and I promised her I'd finish the job today. Are you tellin' me that just because some pin-striped politician who thinks he's in charge tells us we can't travel from A to B, I can't earn a living? Well he can bugger off! I'm off now. You can take my registration number and report me if you like. Ta'ra!' With that he put the van into gear and zoomed off. The policeman switched his radio off and resumed talking to Mandy.

'Sorry about that. It's all very unpleasant but I'm afraid I'm going to ask you to do a U-turn and head home. Can I suggest you watch a recording of the Prime Minister's address to the nation last night?'

He signalled with a twirl of his right arm that the road was clear and as it was quite a wide carriageway there was no need for a three-point turn. That, at least was a blessing, as that manoeuvre wasn't exactly Mandy's strong point.

Forty-five minutes later they were home and dejected. Millie put the kettle on while Jamie fiddled with the TV and BBC i-player.

The words of the Prime Minister on nationwide TV were ominous.

'You must stay at home ….'

Those five little words spoken in just a few seconds were going to have a catastrophic effect on the country for over a year. Millie broke the air of dejection.

'Look, Dad'll be home from Belgium in a couple of days. So, let's go online and take a close look at what suitable properties are on offer. You can bet that in the coming weeks there'll be more and more on the market as folks opt out of the hospitality business. Let's look beyond Brid – what about Filey or even Scarborough? We all liked Scarborough when we did that week there a few years ago didn't we? Well, didn't we?' Lucy perked up.

'Yes! Maybe we could start a donkey-ride business?' Jamie was quick in response.

'You and your animals again. No, we need a business. Millie's right.

Just for once he agreed with his big sister. It was getting serious and they must try and reach some accord before Dad returned from Belgium.

4.

Two hundred miles away on the other side of the North Sea, Peter Fishburn was in a bitter-sweet mood. He had about six hours to play with and wanted to drop in and say cheerio to as many friends and acquaintances as possible. He pondered over a coffee and croissant in the railway station's ornate Brasserie. Smiles and nods of recognition were exchanged with staff members who never seemed to change over the years. There was Anne-Marie, Olga, Natalie and the one he always looked out for first, the lovely Stephanie. Stephanie Van Gelder. He would have to explain to her that their relationship would have to come to an end. She had been his lover and confidante for a decade when the kids were younger and the domestic routine of life in Hull, in between the trips to Belgium, had become boringly soporific. It was his fault and he knew it. Mandy was a lovely girl and had been his school sweetheart since time began but there were only so many times you could take the kids to Hornsea for the day. Hornsea, for God's sake. It wasn't exactly Honolulu was it? He was stirred from his morose daydream by the voice of another waitress, Ena, who had just come on duty.

'Peter, come here. Give me a hug.'

She gave him a peck on both cheeks, Continental style.

'Peter, I've heard bad rumours about the ferry service to Hull. It seems like P & O are winding down their operation here. I hope it doesn't affect your job.' The look on his face said it all.

'It's bad news, Ena. I'm being made redundant. This is my last trip – as a crew member anyway. God only knows when I'll be back. I'm devastated. By the way, have you seen Stephanie?'

Ena smiled to herself. She knew they'd been close, lovers even, and that he often stayed at her apartment in between the phoney 'crew and rota changes' that he'd made up for the family back in Hull. He didn't like telling fibs but Stephanie was something else.

'She's not on duty today, Peter. In fact she might not be in at all. Her brother is very sick and she's trying to run his small restaurant for him in Ostend – The Fleur de Lys. It's almost adjacent to the Mercator Marina. Do you know it?

'No, I don't, but I'm sure I could find it. Where exactly? It's on the right, just past the Titanic Bar. It only has a small frontage so you'll have to keep your eyes skinned.'

That's what Peter loved about the Belgians. They didn't just speak English, they spoke colloquial slang English as well. No chance of the position being in reverse. No Belgian stuck in Hull would be able to find a Flemish speaker within a hundred miles. Peter's brain was racing. Did he have time to get a train to Ostend, only twenty odd kilometres away, to go and say his farewells to Stephanie? This wasn't the case of 'any port in a storm' of the archetypal matelot. Stephanie was extra-special to him. He decided he had to go for it, drained his coffee, and headed for the electronic departure board on the station concourse. His luck was in. The next train to Oostende was due to depart in ten minutes time from Vertrep 10 – platform ten. Purchasing the six Euro ticket from the conveniently quiet booth he walked briskly through the mall of boutiques, chocolate shops and boutiques to Vertrep 10 – the very last one – and jumped onto the moving escalator. There were no more stops between Bruges and Oostende and the electronic board simply flashed Oostende. The silver train came to a halt and the doors opened automatically to disgorge dozens of students heading for the Groene Porte – Belgium's primary college in the field of Hotel Management & Catering. It's reputation was unmatched and students travelled from all over Belgium, including Brussels, to earn the Diploma that would get them a job almost anywhere in Flanders where the hospitality industry reigned supreme.

The train departed exactly on time and Peter grabbed a seat upstairs in the double-decker carriage that was the norm in this part of the country. No need to worry about clearance heights in tunnels in the Low Countries – there simply weren't any. Peter hadn't done this train journey for years but nothing seemed to have changed. They passed Bruges Prison on the left as the suburbs gave way to flat green pastures intersected by a plethora of small streams and bigger canals, some of them huge with flat bottomed cargo barges plying east to enter the commercial network of Belgium's aquatic arteries. Fifteen minutes later and the train pulled into Oostende Station on a platform that looked brand new. The Station had been dramatically upgraded since his last visit some five years ago and now formed part of an interchange between trains, coaches and the famous coastal trams that could take you almost all the way down to Dunkirk. He'd done the 'Kusttram' once with Stephanie and they'd stayed overnight at a small resort called Newport Bad during an unscheduled 'engineering service' that had delayed the return voyage to Hull. That's what he'd told Mandy anyway. Another fib.

'Oostende, Oostende' the electronic voice screamed out, awakening Peter from yet another daydream. He got off the train and headed for the exit and the footbridge that crossed over the canal that led from the North Sea into the Mercator Marina. Across the road he could see a queue of British trippers outside the British Tobacco Shop waiting to buy their maximum allowances of cigarettes, roll-up tobacco and cigars. If those rumours were true then it could be a long time before the shop would be as busy again. Peter crossed over the road and turned left towards the Marina and the forest of yachts' masts that stretched skywards like pine trees with no branches. Turning right this time he soon found the Titanic Bar and then just fifty metres away the Fleur de Lys restaurant. He was gutted. It was closed. On the inside of the attractive glazed door bearing as you would expect, a fleur de lys, was a hand -written note. It was in Dutch and his inadequate linguistic skills let him down. He had a brainwave and photographed the notice with his cellphone. There was little point in staying alone in Ostende. He would only feel even more morose. He retraced his steps to the train station grabbed a coffee from the shiny-new kiosk and walked up to the electronic departures board. The next train, in only fifteen minutes time, was to 'Antwerpen via Brugge' so he was spared having to mull over what might have been. Perhaps it was for the best. Saying goodbye to Stephanie for the last time would have torn his heart in two. On the train he suddenly had a flash and removing his phone from his inside jacket pocket asked the female ticket inspector what the notice in Dutch had read. She spoke excellent English.

'It says – Sorry but we are closed indefinitely due to staff illness and the new Covid Rules coming into force in a few days time.' So that was it. He would never see Stephanie again.

Less than two hours after leaving Bruges he was back there again. Ena was still on duty.

'Well, did you find her? I guess not as if you had done you would not be back here so soon. Coffee?'

'Yes please. Then I think I'll take a walk and go buy some chocolates for the kids. Is Verheecke's still open in Steenstraat? You know, the one with the red and white canopy outside?'

'Of course it is. Some things never change. And don't forget to go see Jerry too. He'll miss you – the amount you spend in there! And don't forget to leave your cellphone number with me.'

Peter made a mental note to do as he was told. Jerry's Cigar Bar was always on the list for the purchase of a carton of Golden Virginia, a small box of Cuban cigars and a couple of packets of Pall Mall menthol cigarettes which he gave to Millie without her Mum knowing. She would have strongly disapproved but it was just another little secret that he shared with the eldest of his offspring. It was a twenty minute walk to Simon Steven Plein almost in the centre of the stunning Medieval City that had often been dubbed 'the Venice of the North' by travel writers.

Jerry and his charming wife Katherine were so pleased to see Peter. It had been a while since his last visit.

'The usual carton of Virginia, a dozen Romeo & Juliet and forty menthol Pall Malls! Yes? Am I right?' They sat down for a coffee and a cognac at one of several tables in front of a massive monochrome depiction of an old square in Havana, Cuba. Jerry poured his heart out to an unawares Peter who slowly began to realise that the Covid pandemic was going to be a trans-European problem. He went on.

'The ferries are running down to crossings every other day from Hull as from the end of the month. As you know much of our business is from Brits like yourself. You should see the amount of Christmas cards we receive every year from Hull and all over Yorkshire. When all this Covid lark is over we must come over and visit your neck of the woods.'

Three hours later and Peter was back on the Pride of Bruges and preparing for his last ever shift with P & O Ferries. It was the end of an era.

5.

The Sunset Lounge was almost full despite the fact that there was still an hour to go before the Pride of Bruges was due to cast off and head back to Hull. There were lots of complaints from some passengers that stocks of tobacco and cigarettes were either low or unavailable in the on-board Duty Free shop. Peter overheard a lot of the conversations and disparaging remarks whilst he was busy serving. It was just as well he had bought his tobacco and cigars at Jerry's in Bruges. Then it occurred to him that the run-down in stock might be deliberate in the company's eyes. All the more reason to suspect that this sector would soon be for the chop. In his break he popped into the shop himself and bought a one litre bottle of Hine cognac for half the normal price which added to his suspicions. You couldn't get much more up-market than Hine and it would be a nice gift for Mandy who liked a tot alongside her Java coffee. His thoughts were interrupted by the 'bing-bong' of the Tannoy system and the deep bass tones of the Dutch master,

'Good evening, my name is Captain Eric Van den Ven. and welcome aboard the Pride of Bruges. The ship is now ready for sea and we shall be leaving the berth in approximately five minutes time.' As he spoke the vibrations below indicated that four of the massive Sulzer marine diesel engines had been started up.

'The weather forecast is for moderate winds from the north-east gusting to Force Four from time to time. We might experience some slight movement so please take care when moving around the vessel. Remember to move your clocks back one hour to British Time. We expect to be on the berth in 'Ull at approximately eight-thirty local time. On behalf of P & O Ferries I wish you a pleasant voyage. Good evening.'

Peter had heard these announcements a thousand times over the last twenty years. His eyes welled up as it dawned on him that he would not hear those words again for a long time, if ever. The shift passed mercifully quickly and by midnight he was back in his crew cabin. He packed up what few personal possessions he had on board. A framed photo of the whole family, including Seb, had been screwed onto the bulkhead for several years. It had been taken on Scarborough's South Bay beach facing north with the remains of the Norman castle high in the background. A passing herring gull had just been caught in the frame, probably en-route to dive bomb an unsuspecting tourist's plate of chips. He wrapped it carefully in a white towel which bore the four-coloured crest of the company's flag in one corner. It would be his one and only souvenir of twenty years service – apart from the redundancy cheque of course. He wondered how long it would be before further details, not to mention the money itself, would arrive.

Peter was awakened just after six-thirty the next morning by a passenger announcement.

'Breakfast is now being served in the Four Seasons Restaurant on Green Deck …'

He settled instead for a coffee and a croissant in the Continental Café on Red Deck where he was able to say final farewells to some of the catering staff which had been drawn in recent years from Eastern European countries and the Philippines. The Captain's estimate of the arrival time had been spot on and just before nine o'clock he disembarked, completed immigration and HM Customs formalities without fuss and and walked into the Arrivals Hall. A familiar voice alerted him and out of the throng of taxi and coach drivers waiting for passengers emerged Millie with the faithful Seb on a lead. He hugged and kissed her on both cheeks and then patted Seb who looked distinctly annoyed that he hadn't come first.

'I got your text that you sent an hour ago so I thought I'd pick you up! We've got a surprise for you. The car's just over the way in the car park. I'm driving.'

'What? Where are we going? Where's Mum and the others?'

'I told you. It's a surprise! Be patient.'

Fifteen minutes later and they were in a 'transport caff ' on the main road towards the Humber Bridge. Lorry drivers were immune from many of the new restrictions and unofficially at least, some 'caffs' were still opening normally to cater for them.

A table for five people had been reserved for them in one corner. The new 'five in a bubble' rule had just come into force. Five 'all day breakfasts' were soon ordered and delivered to the table by a local waitress wearing a blue mask. She looked, and felt, absurd but it was something that they had all better get used to for the next twelve agonising months.

Seb didn't count as a person to break the bubble rule and nestled quietly under the table looking up pitifully at Lucy from time to time. In the end she relented and surreptitiously slipped him one of her sausages under the table. The plates were cleared until only teas and coffees remained on the rustic wooden refectory-style trestle table. Once again it was Millie who took control and she banged her mug on the table to make an announcement. She stared across the table directly into her father's eyes.

'Right, Dad. It's like this. In your absence we have made a family decision. As soon as Mum's inheritance has been received we're selling up here in Hull. We're going to move up the coast and buy a business. We're going to be hoteliers!'

Peter simply didn't know what to say. So he said nowt. Breakfast over, they all piled into the estate and drove home by the shortest route. Thankfully there were no more silly coppers asking silly questions and twenty minutes later they were back in Noseley Way.

Peter unpacked his crew kit-bag, taking care to carefully unroll the P & O towel with the family photo cocooned inside. He wasn't sure what to do with it so he gingerly placed it in his sock draw in the dresser. He would have to decide later what to do with it long term. He sat on the edge of the bed and pondered over what had happened in the last week. Redundancy after two decades service, unemployment, pending poverty, news of an inheritance, separation from a secret lover and now, of all things, the family were insisting that they all became hoteliers. It was too much to take in. He needed to clear his head and decided that a walk in the park with Seb would be a good idea. Seb had already had his first walk of the day but was always up for another and the sound of his lead being jingled as Peter donned his outdoor jacket soon brought him bouncing to the door. Lucy followed him to the porch.

'Don't forget, Dad, under the new rules everyone's only allowed one hour's exercise a day. The Health Minister announced it last night.'

'What? That's just crazy. Well, I suppose if we all do a daily stint then Seb will end up the fittest dog in Hull if he gets five "walkies" every day. Won't he?' Lucy didn't disagree but was already thinking ahead and wondered how the love of her life, until now, would take to paddling in the salt water of Bridlington Bay.

6.

Contrary to the new rules, which millions would take with a pinch of salt anyway, Pete and Seb walked a bit further than he had intended and before he knew it they found themselves at a garden centre near Dunswell. He would get himself a nice cappuccino and a small pack of digestive biscuits which he would share with the ever hungry Seb. Wrong! It was in the process of closing down until further notice and dozens of potted plants including orchids, dwarf palm trees and yuccas were lined up in the car park with a 'Please help yourself' notice propped against the tallest yucca. The management had taken the view that it was better to give them away as an act of goodwill rather than let them perish in the greenhouses which would be devoid of expensive heating for the duration of the lock-down. His mobile screamed in his jacket pocket which caused Seb to bark immediately. It was Mandy.

'Are you coming home for lunch or what? And where are you for goodness sake?'

'I'm at the garden centre near Dunswell. We walked a lot further than we intended but it's done me good. I've cleared my head and maybe even come up with an idea or two. Can Millie come and fetch us?'

Fifteen minutes later Millie pulled up at the centre's car park which was empty save for staff members' cars and a fork-lift truck loading empty wooden pallets onto a small truck. They wouldn't be needed for a while, that's for sure.

'Dad, have you seen that notice over there? Why don't we grab a few small palms and yuccas? We can fold the rear seat down and probably squeeze a few of each in. Seb can get in the front with you.'

'That's being a bit greedy isn't it? I'll just check with the forklift driver first.' He'd already been overheard.

'That's fine pal, take what you want. We must close completely by five o'clock and after that the whole bloody lot will probably go for mulching. Sad but inevitable. The owners will probably claim on their business insurance.'

Lunch was just soup and sandwiches after the big breakfasts they had already had earlier. Mandy was aghast at the mini forest they had brought back with them. Where on earth are we going to put them? Millie always had an answer for everything.

'In the conservatory of course. They might be laying horizontal in the car right now but once upright they'll just tuck in nicely at one end. It'll give us that tropical feeling while we're not allowed foreign holidays. I might even pop back for some more after lunch if there's any left.'

Her mother just scowled but she wasn't the only one who'd inherited those stubborn Viking genes of Eric the Red. By tea time, and two more car-loads, the conservatory was starting to look like an advert for a Caribbean holiday. Millie was streets ahead of the rest of the family but would wait until after tea to broadcast her thoughts. Mentally, she'd been a very busy girl.

The clocks had gone forward the previous weekend to British Summer Time and the lighter nights helped a little to alleviate the air of gloom that descended over the entire nation. How on earth would they cope with weeks of lock-down, or even months if the daily medical statistics didn't improve. Peter drove to the 'chippie' after watching the gloomy six o'clock news and the dreadful daily bulletin from Ministers, SAGE spokesmen and self-appointed experts. The phrase 'next slide please' referring to deaths, hospital admissions and general bad news became an ear worm for millions. The queue outside the Cod and Lobster chippie was twenty yards long as the new 'social distancing' rules had just come into place with ghastly yellow foot-prints painted on the path outside to make people comply. Twenty minutes later and five portions of North Sea cod and chips with two large tubs of mushy peas were in the foot-well of the car. He texted 'five minutes' to Mandy which was his signal to warm the plates and put the kettle on. They couldn't possibly have fish and chips without a pot of Yorkshire Tea – now could they?

With the plates put in the dishwasher all that remained on the table were five mugs, all bearing an image of Seb, which had been a Christmas present to the family from Lucy. She had ordered a set of six but mercifully the sixth one hadn't had to be used yet. Jamie grabbed the huge teapot which had been won on the rifle range at least year's Hull Fair and took it to the kitchen for a fresh brew. A little idea crept into his head but he decided to keep it to himself for the time being.

With a fresh brew on the table and waiting to 'stew' properly as Jamie always called it, once again it was Millie who assumed the role of de facto company chairman. She was getting good at this and was feeling the benefit of her Accountancy & Business Course. She had just started the module on Limited Companies and was streets ahead of the rest of the family. Refilling her mug first, as she didn't like it too strong, she tapped her teaspoon against the side of her mug.

'Order! We all know how difficult life is for everyone in the country at the moment don't we? We have to stay at home most of the time which is just awful. But in addition to doing my coursework I've been using the time to do a lot of research online. Personal viewings of properties is a complete 'no-no' at the moment. And don't forget you'll have to start thinking about putting our house on the market soon too, in fact as soon as lock-down is lifted.' She glanced fleetingly at both her parents who looked a little crestfallen. After all this had been their marital home for twenty years and it was the first, in fact the only home, they had bought and lived in together.

'We'll all have lovely memories of living here, that's for sure. But we must grasp the moment and move forward, all of us. Right, look at these.'

She opened a clear plastic pop-wallet and took out more than a dozen A4 sized photos of small hotels which on the reverse had brief but useful descriptions supplied by the various agents online.

'Here's an example – I'll read it to you.

Small bijou hotel on Bridlington's south promenade. Eight double rooms all with sea views and ensuite. Owners' accommodation to the rear. Licensed. Sufficient parking for six cars. Fifteen minutes walk to the harbour and entertainments. Five year's accounts available upon request from the Agent.

Freehold O.I.R.O. £400,000

She passed it to her mother sat on her left.

'Have a look, Mam, then pass it round.

Here's another one in Filey.

Small boutique B & B on Seashore Road. Six double rooms incorporating a twenty-cover licensed restaurant currently specialising in fresh seafood. Accounts available. Discerning regular clientele.

Freehold. Offers in excess of £500,000. Pass that one round, Mam.'

Four more followed until everyone had one in their hand. It wasn't long before the banter started and the fresh tea was almost forgotten. For the first time young Lucy started to get animated and started waving her sample in the air.

'This one's gorgeous, just look at all those beautiful hanging baskets. And look what else it says – close to golf course and ideal for dog walks – a favourite with dog owners – rated as five-star dog friendly. This is my choice!'

Millie soon brought her sister's joy to an end.

'You've been conned already by the Agent's speel. I've looked on Google Earth and its not far from high cliffs, at least half a mile from a proper road of any kind and would be more suited as kennels rather than a hotel. I'm guessing that's what it used to be.' Lucy looked upset.

'Now, let me show you what I've got here. I've made extra copies of this one so we can all study it at the same time. A simplified breakdown of the last three year's accounts is attached to them.'

They were passed round until everyone had them.

'It's in Scarborough on the North Side. It's currently called the Wendover..

Sixteen bedrooms, all en-suite. Private parking for ten cars plus normally adequate street parking for overflow. Large residents lounge with Bar although the Licence has currently lapsed renewal should not be a problem. Some, mostly cosmetic, redecorating is required. Attractive gardens and sea views to most rooms. Easy access to Peasholm Park and the Open Air Theatre. The Sea Life Centre is either half an hour's walk or ten minutes on the nearby North Bay miniature Railway. The ill-health of the current owners, coupled with the ongoing Covid pandemic, has forced a reluctant sale. POA.'

Jamie was puzzled. 'What does POA mean, Sis?'
'It means Price On Application.'

7.

'**W**ell, what do you all think? Will somebody please say something!'

Her mother opened the batting.

'It sounds gorgeous, just right, but we won't be able to afford that. Surely! It'll be out of our price bracket. But why don't we phone the agents, just out of curiosity if nothing else?'

Millie took another slurp of her tea and smiled inwardly.

'I've already done that! I spoke to a Mr Hopper this morning. A nice man. We had quite a chat actually and he perhaps told me a little more than he should have done about the current owners.'

'Like what?' Said Mandy.

'Well first of all he explained to me that the Wendover was in full flow until the back end of last summer when they had to stop trading. It seems like the owner's wife was in the early stages of dementia without knowing it and when the full diagnosis arrived they ceased trading immediately and put the hotel on the market. The refurbishment and makeover scheduled for the winter months was cancelled of course, hence the wording in the sales speel – cosmetic redecorating required.'

'So how much is for God's sake?' blurted out Mandy. 'Put us out of our misery!'

Millie was in a slightly frivolous mood and decided to play a little game.

'All four of you have to guess and the one nearest to the correct answer can have the biggest slice of the carrot cake I bought earlier at ASDA.' She reached for a pen to write their answers down.

'Dad?' Six hundred thousand.

'Mum?' Seven hundred.

'Jamie?' A million.

'Lucy?'

'That's silly. Come on hurry-up. Seb's waiting for his next walk. It's my turn.'

'Dad's almost spot on. It's on the market for just under six hundred thousand, five nine five to be precise.'

'Wow, that's a surprise but its still out of our price range isn't it? What a shame.' But Millie hadn't finished.

'Not necessarily. Mr Hopper explained that under normal circumstances it would have been snapped up but nothing is normal at the moment is it? There's no sign of lock-down coming to an end any time soon. And as Mr Hopper went on to say – nobody can even view it at the moment. However he told me off the record that his assistant, Rosie, was going to make one of those video viewings within the next few days and he would send it to me before he officially put it up on Zoopla and Rightmove. I told you he was nice!

So, it's a numbers game isn't it? Dad, how much is outstanding on the mortgage here?'

'About thirty thousand from the last statement. It's in the desk somewhere. Why?'

'Well, it's basic arithmetic isn't it? Mum's inheritance is a minimum of four hundred thousand plus the equity in this house so we're only about fifty thousand short, after costs of buying and selling. Aren't we?'

And where do you think that's going to come from? We are not going to use my redundancy cheque, when it bloomin' well comes just to live on. It can't go into the hotel pot either as it were. It's mine and it's going into the bank first.'

The air of positivity started to evaporate. Lucy had had enough and went to get Seb's lead.

'Do want you want. As long as we buy somewhere that's dog friendly.'

She was just about to open the door when she noticed a slim white window envelope on the mat. How long had that been there? Perhaps they had missed it earlier as they had all left by the back door. Curiosity overtook her and she glanced at the addressee and the postmark as she picked it up.

'Dad, there's a letter here for you. It's come first class post and the postmark says Canterbury. I'll put in on the side table. We're off. See ya later.'

Less than a minute later and Peter was poised, knife in hand to slit open the envelope. He knew that it was from the ferry company as they were based in Dover – just down the road from Canterbury. He was nervous and hesitated but was calmed by his wife's soothing tones.

'Come on, love. You might as well find out.' The blade did its job and Pete's fingers trembled as he carefully pulled out a single, folded letter and a cheque. He inadvertently dropped the cheque and it fluttered to the carpet face down, like buttered toast. The next thirty seconds were the longest of his life.

'Well, love. It is my redundancy as this letter explains. It's just under thirty thousand but it's taxable it seems. It hardly seems fair does it? By the time the tax-man's had his slice of it …'

'Don't worry, love, we'll manage.' She held him very close and kissed him on one cheek. It suddenly dawned on Peter how lucky he was to have such a faithful wife and supportive family. He chided himself inwardly. How could he possibly have taken a mistress in Belgium when all this love and devotion was only two hundred nautical miles away?

They all had lovely, expectful dreams that night. Lucy walked Seb to the Sea Life Centre in Scarborough. Jamie raced his new motorbike around the Marine Drive in the middle of the night. Pete and Mandy hosted a 'Welcome open evening' at the Wendover Hotel. Millie slept soundly without any dreams, as she recalled. She alone in the family knew they had a long way to go. Mr Hopper had also informed her that even if they had all the money available and an offer was accepted, the Land Registry was in a state of chaos. Too many staff were either sick or working from home. They were all in for a long haul. But Millie did keep one card up her sleeve that she kept to herself. She had spoken to her course Tutor, a Mr Clive White, who was a retired bank manager. What he told her about one particular item in that Schedule of Assets in the solicitor's communication to her mother, would make even Yul Bryner's hair curl. She could recall the telephone conversation almost word for word.

'The Hudson Bay Trading Company did you say, Millie? Now that's interesting.

'Really? Why?'

'Well I remember an almost identical scenario, oh maybe ten years ago, or more even. We held lots of locked deed boxes for safe-keeping in our strongrooms. A firm of solicitors phoned up one day to say that a member of their staff would be coming to collect the box as our customer had died. They were Executors for the deceased. Once opened, the box apparently contained lots of share certificates including one of the Hudson Bay Trading Co. Our mutual client had been a Master Mariner and had spent a lot of his time trading between Liverpool and Halifax, Nova Scotia. He was a lot wealthier than anyone had realised. Anyway the long and short of it was that it took months to get a Probate value for those shares. Bearer shares are tricky as the annual dividends can be claimed by anybody who actually bears the shares in their hands at the time – hence the name Bearer shares. On the back of the certificate are dozens of what resemble large postage stamps with serrated edges. Each stamp is for a particular year 2000, 2001, 2002 and so on. Every year the holder of the share certificate peels off the 'stamp' for that year and sends it off to the Registrars.

'Who are they exactly then?'

'The Registrars, usually a bank, are the Trustees and its their job to ensure that the shareholders get their annual dividends.'

'So what happens if nobody claims the dividends? Are they just lost?'

'No, that's what I'm just coming to. If they're unclaimed they just go on deposit at the bank until they are eventually claimed. In our case they hadn't been claimed since just after the Second World War, can you believe that? The final total, when it was eventually received, was almost a half a million Canadian dollars – a quarter of a million sterling. The sole beneficiary was a nineteen year old grandson of the deceased who was an apprentice mechanic at a garage in Wincolmlee. He nearly had a cardiac arrest when the solicitor broke the news to him. But, Millie, be cautious. Until Hymers solicitors locate the certificate from Barclays it's only guesswork. Anything else I can help you with?'

'No thanks, Mr White, but nearer the time we'll need advice about opening a business account at a suitable bank.'

'You'll be lucky, there are hardly any proper banks left now after the latest wave of closures due to Covid. You know what banks are like – any excuse to close a branch down!'

He was right there.

8.

Weeks turned into months and the entire nation was cheesed off – to put it mildly! It was not natural for millions to stay at home. The daily briefings from Downing Street became even more repetitive and boring. People who were old enough to remember the brilliant comedian called it 'Hancock's Half Hour' whenever the Health Secretary made an appearance which, sadly, was most days. But slowly the restrictions on social activities started to be made less severe. Folks could go out in family groups and gatherings called bubbles. Millions received a jab in one or both arms as vaccines were rolled out across the nation and of course the Government took the credit. Don't they always?

Millie was continuing with her online course in Accountancy and Business and was surprised to receive a small income known as 'furlough' as the motel she had worked in was closed for several months. Jamie and Lucy's schools were both closed and it was beginning to look as if they wouldn't reopen until after the summer holidays.

In July the country started to open-up again and people were allowed to travel within so many miles from home. Millie, once again, took charge.

'Right, we've all seen the video viewing of the Wendover Hotel in Scarbados, er I mean Scarborough. So lets book an appointment to view it with that Mr Hopper.'

She had almost given the game away with her idea. So fixated had she become with the idea of moving to

Scarborough that every morning she had taken to the idea of listening to BBC Radio York on DAB radio from seven until ten. She set her radio alarm for six-forty five, made tea and took it back to bed. She had done this since lockdown had started, so convinced was she that for the family's prosperous future, that just had to move from Hull to Scarborough.

The morning presenter was called Georgey, full of fun and wit. She had both in bucketfuls but you probably had to, starting that early in the morning. Each day a topic was chosen and listeners were invited to email, text or WhatsApp their opinion to the central studio in York. One morning recently Georgey asked her thousands of listeners – 'What's the most embarrassing thing that ever happened to you at work?'

Georgey always selected a few to read out on air including this one:

'Morning Georgey. On my first day at a new Branch of my bank in Hull, a member of staff returning from her lunch break pointed to a security button and said 'let me in please – press that button there.' There were two buttons and of course I pressed the wrong one. It was the main alarm linked to Humberside Police HQ half a mile away in Queens Gardens. Three police Ford Granadas arrived within two minutes. I was in deep poo.' Mark in Scarbados.

It was those last words – Mark in Scarbados – that caught Millie's attention. It so obviously wasn't a slip of the tongue. Some wordsmith had made it up. Millie never, ever forgot.

July arrived and people started to travel a bit more. Beaches were once again packed with folks who had resented being cooped up at home like battery hens.

It was time to actually travel to Scarborough and take a proper viewing of the Wendover Hotel. In reality would it live up to expectations? Everybody knew what property agents were like and camera angles could be used to good effect to make small rooms look large and a distant ocean appear to be a stone's throw away.

With Mum and Dad's approval and blessing, a call was put in to the nice Mr Hopper and arrangements were made to have a proper viewing the following Saturday at eleven o'clock. They all hoped it would be a fine day. The seaside always looks at its best when the sun's shining.

Saturday duly arrived and after a hearty breakfast they all piled into the estate. Seb was not happy to be relegated to the rear behind a steel mesh dog guard. What had he done to deserve this?

Problems started when they hit heavy traffic as soon as they reached the turn-off for Hornsea. Mandy was not best pleased – as they say in Yorkshire.

'I told you, we should avoid the coast road, Pete. It's mayhem. Every man and his dog wants to see the sea after being locked up!'

'On no you didn't! When?'

'You never listen. The traffic will be even worse as we get nearer to Brid. I told you!'

There was no point in arguing with a female Viking. Over the last twenty years Pete had come to realise that. They were *always* right. At least spending all that time at sea or in Belgium had given him respite On the back seat Millie was fiddling with her iPhone, the latest model of course. She lived with it and slept with it.

'I'm calling Mr Hopper out of courtesy to tell him we'll be running late.' He gave them some advice and local knowledge. Millie switched her phone onto speaker mode so they could all hear, especially Pete who was driving.

'Hi everyone. It's Charlie Hopper here. Look it's my fault, I should have told you being unused to North Yorkshire. Firstly, ignore your satnav if you have it switched on. It will probably take you on a guided tour of every coastal mile. In fact switch it off! Take the next turning you see for Driffield and head west. Keep the sun behind you and turn north when you reach the Driffield ring-road. Take the B1249 to Scarborough. If you see a sign for RAF Staxton Wold you know you're on the right road. Got it?' Pete was so relieved. At last a man was doing the navigating.'

'Thanks Mr Hop, er Charlie. Much obliged.' Mandy was still scowling.

'Look, call me again as you come into Scarborough as soon as you go past LIDL's on your left. I'll give you directions from there. OK?'

'Roger and out.' Just for a second Pete thought he was back on the Pride of Bruges. Those were the days but those days would never return.

Just under an hour later and they found themselves on the outskirts of Scarborough and crawling along at ten knots, according to Peter anyway.

'Look there's LIDL's on the left. Millie call that Mr Hopper,' But Millie was already onto it. She was on the ball.

'Right, keep going on this road until you pass a church on your right by some traffic lights. Go past a big petrol station on your left and approach the lights in the left hand lane. Do not follow the sign that says North Bay attractions. You'll end up in the town centre. Turn left onto the A170 for four hundred yards and you'll see a big white pub ahead of you – the Crown Tavern. Drive into the car park and I'll see you there in five to ten minutes. I'm in a black BMW. See you soon.'

They rendezvoused in the pub car park without difficulty. Mr Hopper wound down his window as the two cars drew parallel.'

'Welcome to Scarborough! Boy, is it busy today or what? Just follow me. You might think we're going nowhere but the traffic is unbelievable and I'm going to take us via a slightly circuitous route to try and avoid the worst of it. Right, follow me.'

They turned left and then left again onto what appeared to be the main road to Whitby, the A171. After a mile or so the BMW indicated to turn right at some traffic lights.

'This is Green Lane' uttered Jamie who had switched on a map App on his mobile. ' We're heading east towards the sea. I can see it ahead. Look! So they all did.

More traffic lights and yet another right turn. Suddenly on their left appeared the huge yellow structure of Alpamare – a new aquatic park that had been somewhat controversial when it was first mooted, let alone built.

'Wow, that's new since we were last here' observed Mandy. 'It looks massive doesn't it? I bet that gets very busy once all the Covid restrictions are over.'

The road dropped slowly down almost to sea level and they passed the engine sheds of the miniature railway mentioned in the sales brochure. Next on the left was the entrance to one of Scarborough's prime attractions and the envy of almost every other resort in England – The Open Air Theatre, known locally as the OAT. It was the jewel in Scarborough's crown and attracted top artistes from around the globe. The 'beamer' started to indicate right again and the sylvan setting of Peasholm Park appeared below to the left as they climbed a modest hill for no more than two hundred yards. Lucy spotted it first.

'Look! There it is. The Wendover. Doesn't it look lovely?' The sun had just come out and the pale cream facade of the hotel positively glowed. The palm trees around the front door rippled in welcome in the slight breeze from the sea. The omens could not have been better.

9.

The car park was big and tarmacked and every bit as described in the brochure, as they say. It was flaking a bit at the edges but nothing that a travelling tarmacker with a hot wheelbarrow and a shovel couldn't put right in an hour and fifty quid cash in hand. Mr Hopper immediately assumed his role as Negotiator.

'Right, welcome to the Wendover. The Hotel hasn't been occupied for well over six months now so the first thing I have to do is switch off the alarm system and then quickly sanitise all the door handles with this here squirty anti-bacterial stuff. Just give me five minutes please. Why don't you all look all round the outside while I'm doing that? As you you can see the rear garden extends back a long way up to that laurel hedge which keeps it quite private. Anyway, just have a nosey round and I'll give you a shout when to come in OK?'

Seb had beaten them all to it having already bounded down to the far end of the garden. It was a whole new world for him of new smells and surroundings. He cocked his leg against a small tree that had obviously not been attended to for some time. The garden, which was mostly lawn, obviously needed more than a little TLC, certainly more than the hourly paid temporary gardener arranged by the Agent had given it. The faded stripes of the grass looked more like a marrow past its sell by date than a tiger's arse.

A shout from the door of the conservatory overlooking the garden brought them back to attention.

'Right, you're free to go into any of the rooms and all door handles are sanitised for your safety. I'm going to nip outside for a quick fag.' Millie wished she could join him but kept her thoughts to herself. In any case her menthol Pall Malls were back in Hull. Damn!

They split into two groups, Mum and Dad started upstairs and worked their way down. There was a lot to see. On the second floor and built into the eves, were four bedrooms, a massive double room with an en-suite and three single bedrooms which shared a family bathroom. Mandy was impresed.

'I'd guess this is the owner's accommodation at the top here. Well so far it ticks all the boxes doesn't it? Three single rooms and three kids – it couldn't be better. Both bathrooms need a bit of upgrading but nothing too serious. Let's move down.'

It was even better news. Most of the en-suites looked almost new. In fact two of the glass shower screens were still covered in the factory-fitted polythene sheath with 'fragile' in red stickers plastered across them. On the ground floor it was a slightly different story. The cosy resident's lounge looked like one of those reminiscence rooms that are often found in nursing homes. Fifties style curtains and carpets took you back over half a century and you could almost hear the opening bars of Coronation Street and Ena Sharples if you tried hard. It was a not dissimilar story in the dining room and the half-dozen wooden ceiling lights looked as if they belonged to a world of austerity with at least half the bulbs missing in each unit. It was a big room though and easily accommodated the dozen or so small tables which could be set for one, two or even four people at a pinch. The kitchen was large with a useful pantry and a 'chill room' with two large upright freezers. Two 'Rangemaster' ovens were fitted and looked almost new on close inspection. A utility room with ultra-modern washers and driers completed the downstairs accommodation. Hopper assumed his role once again.

'Well, that's it, warts and all. I don't think we've exaggerated anything in the brochure. It does need some cosmetic upgrading I'll give you that but nothing that can't be sorted. I think it needs to be looked at with a different perspective than the previous owners. I understand they catered mainly for what is often unkindly called the 'grey brigade' – you know, Seniors with a few bob who liked the sea air but dismissed the South Side of town with its, to them anyway, vulgar amusement arcades, bingo and chip shops. To me the North side of town is the future and the acts attracted to the OAT are just getting more and more mind-blowing. Next year, when Covid is truly over, I think we can expect to see the sort of acts and artists coming here that you would normally expect at places like the O2 Arena in London. So, at six-nine-five I think the Wendover is a snip and it's only the current situation in the country that is depressing the price. In a year or two its market value could be top a million and …'

'Thank you, Mr Hopper. We've got a lot to discuss and think about' said Pete. Of course he hadn't mentioned that it was his wife's inheritance that would be paying, let alone that it would be months before the brass was in the bank. Unusually, Millie said absolutely nothing.

The drive back to Hull was unhurried and this time they did take the 'scenic route' firstly right around the Marine Drive to the South Bay, past the Luna Park and the crab stalls, the harbour itself and the brand new award winning

RNLI boathouse. The lifeboat itself was on the beach on a tracked low-loader being towed back from the water's edge by a specially designed tractor that looked as if it would be equally happy underwater.

'Dad, can we stop for an ice cream please?' said Lucy.

'Only if we can get parked. It's manic isn't it?' He turned left onto the West Pier and spotted a transit van that looked as if it had seen better days pull out. The driver looked a bit rough with both arms heavily tattooed but as drew level he wound his window down and proffered a small piece of paper towards Peter.

'Ere y'are mate. There's an hour left unexpired on this parking ticket. No point in wasting it. Best nip in there before some other bugger spots it.' How kind and totally unexpected. As they drove past, the cocker spaniel in the back spotted Seb and they exchanged howls for a few seconds. Safely parked and the donated ticket placed securely above the dashboard, they all got out and Seb was placed on a lead. Three 'ninety-nines' and two 'lemon-tops' were soon acquired from the famous Harbour Bar and all was well with the world.

'It doesn't seem five minutes since we were last here does it, love? But do you know it's actually more than five years?' He didn't mention the framed photo he had saved from his cabin on the Pride of Bruges. That would come as a surprise later at a time of his choosing. No rush.

For the next hour they ambled along the front to where a giant Ferris wheel had replaced the Futurist Theatre, another Scarborough icon that had been consigned to history. But it didn't bother the Fishburns a jot. They were confirmed North Siders now. All they needed was the wonga to come through and an offer to be accepted.

On the coastal road home via Bridlington all the chatter was about the Wendover and how that could make it work in their eyes. Millie, sat in the rear with her siblings, was deep in thought and had switched her iPhone to calculator mode. She knew something the others didn't and she didn't dare spill the beans. An old school friend, Sharon, had accepted a bona-fide apprenticeship to a firm of solicitors in Hull. Hymers to be precise. Two hours earlier and she had sent a WhatsApp message to her mate with information that would have got her dismissed if it ever came to light. That's why she used the encrypted WhatsApp programme. It was short and to the point:

'Hudson Bay has come up trumps. Letter in post. See ya soon. Shazza x.'

An hour later and they pulled into Noseley Way. The ever maternal Mandy was first into the kitchen to put the kettle on for a brew of Yorkshire Tea.

'Pete, pick the post off the mat, love. Looks like deliveries are starting to get back to normal again.'

10.

Once Mandy had recognised the Hymer & Hymer franking mark on the envelope it took her only thirty seconds to open the regular sized deluxe window envelope. The tea was momentarily forgotten. She sat at the kitchen table and read it slowly to herself to take it all in. It was only a single page on this occasion.

Dear Mrs Fishburn

In the matter of the late Mary Mildred Leonard

We write to you, once again, with what I trust you will find two welcome pieces of news.

Firstly, I can report that a cash offer has been made for 'Skylark Cottage' in the village of Preston in the quantum of two hundred and fifty thousand pounds. You will recall that this was the sum we had previously estimated under the Schedule of Assets. This will therefore be the Probate valuation when the time comes.

Secondly, I am delighted to tell you that the problem of the valuation of the Hudson Bay Trading Company Bearer Shares has also been concluded. Upon receipt of the relevant certificate from Barclays it was scanned and forwarded to the Registrars in Toronto. The company has undergone complex corporate restructuring in the last decade with part sales of some of its Divisions to other companies. However, the salient point is that many years of dividends remained unclaimed which were deposited in interest bearing accounts – thirty two years to be precise. Allowing for a currency conversion rate of one dollar and sixty-six cents (Canadian) as at the date of death the value of the holding is approximately six hundred and forty two thousand pounds sterling. This came as much of a shock to us as I'm sure it will to you too. This will be verified as soon as the certificate itself has been sent by courier to Toronto.

This then values the total Estate at just over one million pounds. In my previous communication I didn't mention IHT (Inheritance Tax) which must now form a necessary part of the equation in view of the quantum involved. Tax due to the Exchequer will thus be slightly in excess of two hundred and seventy thousand pounds leaving an approximate net value of the estate at seven hundred and thirty thousand. Allowing for the three bequests to animal charities your net legacy will thus be in the order of seven hundred thousand.

As Executors we can now shortly begin to proceed with application to the Probate Court but we must advise you that our current estimates are that it will take four months to complete the process and we thus cannot see distribution taking place much before early to mid November.

We will of course be in touch in the interim if need be and please do not hesitate to contact me if you have any queries.

Yours etc.

Mandy read the letter again and started to weep. Everybody read the letter in turn except Millie who was busy brewing the tea in the kitchen. Had she read it she would have recognised the reference JH/SEM at the top. At the very least she owed her mate Sharon Elizabeth Mason a gin or two – when the clubs and pubs opened properly again anyway.

'Well, what's our next step then?' remarked Pete who passed his wife a sheet of kitchen roll to dry her eyes. 'We've got to play it cool with that Hopper guy.'

'Yes we do, but how cool? We firstly have to decide as a family if we want to buy it. Do we all agree to leaving Hull where we have lived all our lives? It will be a huge emotional rift and are we experienced enough to make a success of it?' There was silence from almost all of them until Lucy, the youngest, broke the silence.

'I say let's go for it! And Seb just loved it didn't he? He just loved that garden the second he got out of the car.'

'What do you think, Jamie' who looked impassive and a little sad.

'On the assumption I pass my bike test soon, I say let's go. I'll be able to come back and see my mates at weekends whenever I want to. The roads won't be too busy in the winter and I'll have time on my hands to zip back here and...'

'Oh no you won't little brother. Not if my plans come to fruition.'

And with that she threw an A4 lever arch file onto the coffee table narrowly missing the milk jug and five mugs. On the cover in large, bold red letters were four words:

HOTEL SCARBADOS
Business Plan

The others were speechless. Gob-smacked as they say in Yorkshire. Mandy reacted first.

'Oh my God, Millie. What on Earth is this and just where did you get that crazy name from? It's absolutely horrendous!'

Both Jamie and Lucy didn't agree with her. Jamie shouted first.

'Well I tell you what, Sis, I think it's brill. Great. Scarborough and Barbados all rolled into one word.'

He did his best to imitate a well know hotel booking agency that advertised a lot on TV.

'Hotel...Scarbados. Hotel....Scarbados. Yes, it just rolls off the tongue doesn't it? What do you think, Dad?'

'Mmm, well I guess I could get used to it. Maybe it'll grow on me. He too repeated the mantra several times. 'D'ya know it's actually quite catchy.' Mandy knew she had to relent and once again Millie took the reins.

'I've checked there are no other hotels with the same name. We'll be unique. It gives us the opportunity to create a warm, welcome atmosphere all the year round. And did you notice those gorgeous palm trees at the front? Now you know why Dad and I acquired those extra ones when the garden centre temporarily closed down. They can be planted either down the side of the drive or at the back. It'll add extra privacy, won't it?' Her Mother interrupted.

'So exactly how long have you been planning this, Millie ? It's all a bit presumptive on your part isn't it? And where did you get the name from? Did you make it up?'

'No, I didn't but somebody else did. I've been listening to BBC Radio York for months. There's a guy from Scarborough who regularly contributes anecdotes and quips to the early morning show and his handle is *Mark in Scarbados*. It just struck a chord with me and I kept it up my sleeve until now. So are we all agreed then? Mum, it's your money – when it arrives – so you should have the final word. And in any case the Wendover Hotel hardly has a ring to it does it? Once you've seen Hotel Scarbados on a website you'll never forget it. Well?' All eyes were on Mum.

'Come to think of it, it does have a sort of catchy ring to it doesn't it. OK let's go for it but don't forget, we haven't actually bought it yet and although we know from the solicitors that it's only a matter of time we mustn't count our chickens, as they say.'

The Six o'clock News on TV brought an unwelcome development.

'Good evening, the headlines and main news tonight. Covid cases have spiked again at an alarming rate and the Government is reintroducing more restrictions. The general thinking is that previous rules and restrictions were relaxed too soon. Overseas travel is once again being severely curtailed and thousands of Brits away on holiday are desperately trying to get flights home ..'

Millie just smiled. It was all the more reason for buying a nice hotel on UK soil and making it work all the year round. Young Jamie had another think coming if he thought all his weekends would be 'off' and he'd be zooming back to watch Hull City every other Saturday.

After tea they all sat in the lounge and despaired at the latest news and the return of restrictions. Peter had brought Millie's lever-arch file through and waived it above his head.

'So, what's in here then? You act as though you've just won that 'The Apprentice' programme on TV with Sir Alan what's his face.'

'You mean Lord Sugar?'

'Yes, him. Well I do actually watch that programme even if you don't. And for your information a girl from Hull did actually win it once. You can learn a lot from that show and …'

'So, what's in this fancy file then? Jargon and buzz-words like market forces, asset ratios and the like?'

'Open it and see for yourself, Dad. Go on.' So Pete did just that.

'It's empty. What are you playing at?'

'No, it's not. Look again.'

'Oh right, I see now. Loads of subject dividers.' He counted them. 'Eight!

'Now look at the labels on the top of each one. Read them out, Dad.'

'Banking arrangements. Computers. Card readers. Website. Insurances. Removals. Alarms and Fire Certificates. Advertising. Wow! You have been busy.'

'On the contrary. We can't tackle many of those points until we have a completion date for the purchase but we can make provisional plans for the advertising and the website – on the assumption we will eventually get possession and actually move in. So let's get our thinking caps on shall we?'

11.

It was almost midnight by the time they had finished chatting, with Millie taking notes of course. She didn't tell them that part of her course in recent days had involved setting up a theoretical business. It could have applied to any small business – even a pet shop or a fish and chip shop. Later in the course they would cover Limited Companies but that would be next year.

'So, I'll check-out the availability of a suitable website. Dad, if you and Jamie can start thinking about the actual move itself, you know, what we're taking and what we're leaving. Not to mention booking a suitable removal company once we can get a moving date.'

'Yes, I know a guy from Brid who comes highly recommended. James somebody. I've got it written down somewhere.' That's her Dad's problem Millie thought to herself. He always had something put somewhere safe. But could he ever find anything?

'Mum, I thought you and Lucy could concentrate on the domestic side of things. You know, figure out what we need to buy when we do move.'

'Really, like what?' exclaimed Mandy. All the fixtures and fittings are included in the price – if we go ahead. What if it falls through? We haven't even made a formal bid yet, let alone had it accepted.'

'Well yes but those huge freezers and fridges are empty and switched off with all the doors left slightly ajar. They'll have to be stocked if only for our own use. And of course when we open we'll open a Trade account with a suitable cash and carry.'

Millie slept well that night. Things were moving, albeit slowly. What they needed now was to make an offer and get it accepted. After that that things would start to slide into place – hopefully.

Shortly after breakfast the next morning during which an opening offer was mutually decided upon, Peter called Charles Hopper at the agents. He had just lit a fag and was halfway through his third black coffee of the morning. Times were hard and if the Covid regulations weren't eased soon then although properties could be viewed, actually moving in could be a while. What was the point in purchasing if you couldn't move in? The 'chains' as agents called them, were getting longer. With a lack of sales, agents were starting to feel the pinch too. Hopper answered his phone on the second ring.

'Oh hello Mr Fishburn, good to hear from you.' With luck some good news was about to arrive.

'We've had an update from the solicitors here in Hull. He says that with luck Probate will be granted by early to mid November. So on that basis we'd like to put an offer in to the vendors via your good-self.'

'Well that is good news, Mr Fishburn. The asking price is six-nine-five as you know. So shall we go in with an opening offer of say six-seven-five and try and save you you a few grand?'

'Er no, we'll go in with an opening offer of six forty-five.' At the other end of the line Hopper almost choked on his Park Lane.

'What?! Well to be honest I don't think they'll accept it. Why don't we try six...'

'No. With respect we're doing the bidding not you. We appreciate that you have a duty to your best for your clients but our offer stays at six forty-five. Put that to the vendors please and get back to me today if you possibly can. We're eager to complete. Thank you.' Peter hung up. Millie positively beamed.

'Well done, Dad, you were brilliant. It was just like watching *A Place in the Sun* where they do the bidding bit right at the end. I'd love to be a fly on the wall in Hopper's office.'

Fifty miles north, in his down-town Scarborough office, things were going from bad to worse for Charlie Hopper. His cigarette had gone out while he was on the phone to Peter Fishburn so he removed a fresh one from a pack in his jacket pocket. He was spitting feathers.

'You know Rosie, that Hull family I showed round the Wendover Hotel a few days ago?'

'That lot with three kids and a dog right? You told me about them.'

'Yeah, that lot, bloomin fish-heads if you ask me. Anyway the cheeky sods are only offering six hundred and forty five thousand against an asking price of six nine five.'

'Oh no! Didn't you arrange a special deal with the vendors? You know fifty ….'

'Yeah, our commission is normally a fixed one per cent but on this occasion its one percent on the first six-fifty and fifty per cent on anything over that. He seems stuck on that offer from the tone of his voice.'

'But you said they all loved it – even the dog!'

'Well the dog didn't even go inside but I saw it have its first wee in North Yorkshire at the bottom of the garden. It looked at home already. The vendors are already in Spain or Tenerife or wherever to avoid Capital Gains Tax. They gave us carte-blanche to accept any offer over six hundred grand. Shall I play hard-ball and try and get a bit more from these people?'

'To be honest, Mr Hopper, I wouldn't. Once Hull people dig their heels in that's it. Stubborn as hell from my experience. What was that joke about Hull, Hell and Halifax …'

'Yes, all right I take your point. I'll wait an hour or so to make it look like we're doing our job properly.'

'The other thing is Mr Hopper, we really need the six thousand plus commission it will generate anyway don't we? Two more residential sales fell through this morning. Did I tell you? Both taken off the market until early next year – Covid reasons again. At least this Hull lot are cash buyers. Would you like me to call Mr Fishburn back when you're at lunch? '

'Would you? Thanks. Tell him I'm out on business, even if I'm not. The usual speel. In fact I think I'll take a half-day as there's almost nothing doing is there?'

'You can say that again. Leave it with me. See you tomorrow. I'll call you if anything crops up OK?'

Back in Hull, Millie had made coffee for her and her Dad. And their favourite ginger biscuits. It was a freshly opened packet and from twenty feet away Seb could already smell the unique aroma of the spice you either loved or hated. They were Seb's favourite too and he looked longingly at Millie until she relented and proffered half a biscuit towards his nose. He looked mightily disappointed that Millie ate the other half. Now Lucy would not have done that he thought to himself. Lucy was his favourite as she always carried some doggie treats in her anorak pocket and she always gave him one after after every call of nature. So he peed a lot. She hadn't cottoned on yet.

'I don't think Hopper will wait all that long, Dad. The vendors are already living in Lanzarote and they've almost certainly given the agent authority to negotiate within certain limits.'

'What? How can you be so sure?'

'Didn't you notice those pamphlets on that side table in the entrance hall of the Wendover Hotel when we looked round? Loads of them. Some had been downloaded and printed off, you could tell. Others were glossy ones that obviously came by air-mail. But that was many months ago before they vacated the premises. And they certainly didn't live there all the time did they, that's for sure. The so-called owners' accommodation hadn't been properly lived in for a long time. My guess is that they had another house, maybe close-by, that they owned and lived in. Not short of brass I'm telling you. They will accept our offer but when the Hopper chap comes back he'll say that he had a job to persuade them to come down to our offer price but …' Right on cue Pete's mobile phone rang. He switched it to 'speaker' mode so that Millie could listen in.

'Hello, Mr Fishburn? Hi, it's Mr Hopper's secretary speaking. He asked me to call you as he's been delayed on a big valuation project at a new housing estate just out of town. Anyway it's good news. The vendors have just called from Lanz … er abroad, where they have taken up residence. They have reluctantly agreed to your offer on condition that the sale definitely completes in this tax year. So if you'd like to inform your solicitors then things can get weaving, subject to the remaining Covid restrictions of course.'

'That's wonderful. Thank you. We will be proceeding as quickly as possible. In any event we would like to be moved in by Christmas, all things being equal. We'll be in touch, or rather our solicitors will. Thanks again. Goodbye.' Pete hung up.

'What did I tell you Dad? They're in Lanzarote and are obviously keen to minimise Capital Gains Tax. According to my tutor, Mr White, all these type of agents are full of shit and ...'

'Language, young lady, language. You'll have to mind your P's and Q's when we start trading. What about some elocution lessons to iron out that East Hull twang you've got?'

Millie just glared at him – as daughters do.

12.

Things were moving along apace now and the family decided to use the same firm of solicitors in Hull that were handling Aunt Mary's estate to handle the purchase of the Wendover Hotel. After all there were no 'conflicts of interest' involved and in any event they didn't know any solicitors in Scarborough. Charles Hopper sent them an email to say he could recommend a firm in Scarborough who were very friendly and efficient. 'I'll bet he can' thought Millie with Mr White's cautions echoing in her mind.

'There'll have been a kick-back involved of some kind I reckon, Dad. Don't you?'

'Who knows but your Mr White has been so helpful already and we haven't even exchanged contracts to buy it yet, let alone moved in.'

Millie was mentally ticking off the 'List of Eight' as she dubbed it.

'Oh Dad, I forgot to mention your redundancy cheque. Because it's less than thirty thousand it will be tax-free – one less thing for you to be concerned about. It's all yours so when we've moved, and assuming the money isn't needed for the business, you might like to think about putting it all into Premium Savings Bonds.'

'You mean Ernie?'

'Yes! With that sort of amount you could probably look forward to a prize every other month – even if it's only twenty-five quid. Why not? And who knows you might even land the big one! And it's risk free. You can cash them in any-time. Wait until we've moved in, then the National Savings Office in Sunderland will have your correct address from the start.'

Where would they all be without Millie, mused Pete. Bloomin' nowhere that's where. If it wasn't for her and her dynamic ideas what would he be doing now? Signing on for benefits probably and scanning the 'Jobs Vacant' columns. He had watched that movie I, Daniel Blake directed by Ken Loach a few years earlier and a chill went through him. A man who couldn't find a job and didn't have the computer skills to even search for one, was left in the mire by the system. Thank goodness for his eldest daughter, a charming, smart and educated girl who epitomised the 21st century. Her online course was perfect for the situation they had found themselves in. What a good job she had chosen Accountancy & Business and not Media Studies or Hairdressing. He came out of his daydream.

'Dad, we must assume that everything will go to plan over the next few weeks. Time's marching on.' She had purchased a "no frills" calendar from WH Smith – no pictures of birds, dogs or castles – just a blank line for each day. In fact she had also bought the same type for next year as well and had provisionally written OPEN in red letters just before Easter, in fact Maundy Thursday to be precise. Assuming all the Covid restrictions were lifted in full then, with a following wind, they would be open for business.

'Now Dad, another thing, we have to seriously consider banking arrangements. According to Mr White it's not nearly as easy as it used to be. Neither you, Mum nor I have had business accounts before. Apparently long since gone are the days when you just walked into the "Dogger Bank" and told the clerk you wanted a new account. It seems like most of the old-established banks look for a reason *not* to open you a new account and not the other way round. And loads of people who've been with their existing banks are even getting 'de-banked' apparently – just because they don't approve of what you do. It's a new phenomenon that's just come out of the blue.

'So, what's the answer? Does Mr …'

'Yes, he says to ignore the mainstream High Street Banks and to go for one of the newish online Banks who are bending over backwards to attract new SME's like us and …'

'A what? Sorry love but I'm just a redundant ferry steward. You're streets ahead of me.'

'Sorry Dad, I'll try to use ordinary language. SME stands for Small Medium Enterprise. The country's economic backbone is built on SME's. Far more folks own or work for these small businesses that all your ICI's and BP's put together. Trust me.'

'So did he come up with a name?'

'Yes, you might have seen them advertise on TV. They're called the Blackbird Bank and because it's all done online they've been largely unaffected by the Covid epidemic. And one thing's for sure …'

'What's that?'

'Well they won't be closing any Branches down because they haven't got any!'

'So how do we proceed?'

'I'll make enquiries but as soon as we get a completion date we'll start. Speaking of dates in that respect I think you or Mum should speak to Mr Hymer again. And did you make provisional arrangements with James, the removal man?'

'Er, no. But I have found his number. I listed it in small address book in the bureau but I did it wrong. Seems like

James is his surname which fooled me – it's Clayton James. He's based in Brid.'

'Well that's quite handy then. Give him a call over the next few days and ask him to come and see what we've got to actually move on the day. He'll draw up an itinerary and hopefully give us a quote. Just do it!'

Peter did as Millie asked within half an hour. She was working damned hard on everything and he didn't want to appear lax. Mr James' mobile rang as he was driving one of his removal vehicles up the AI towards Newcastle-upon-Tyne. Fortunately he had a blue tooth hands-free connection.

'James' Removals – how can I help you. Hull to Scarborough did you say? Restrictions haven't been totally removed yet, you do know that don't you? So you can't have a date fixed yet. Business is terrible. Today I'm just moving some stuff to a warehouse in Gateshead – me and the lad. No other humans involved. Mind you, I've heard rumours of a 'window' when the Government says that people can move house, subject to all sorts of health restrictions of course. These are terrible times for the housing market I'm sure and it's causing problems every time a chain is broken. The Wendover did you say? Actually I know it. The whole family had a long weekend near there before all this Covid lark. It's near the old swimming pool isn't it?'

'Er really. I didn't notice it, I have to say.'

'No that's because the Council knocked it down and built another one in a new sports village nowhere near the sea. Anyway, I know roughly where it is. And exactly where are you in Hull? Not anywhere near the Land of Green Ginger I hope. I got charged with obstruction the last time I moved someone there – I couldn't find anywhere else to park. That's Humberside Police for you.'

'No, we're in Noseley Way in Kinsgwood and …'

'Just send me a text with your street number and postcode and I'll find you. I'll drive down one evening and give you a quote. Anyway, I'm just about to pull off the A1 now so I'll sign off. Bye.'

'That was short and sweet, Dad. What did he say?'

'He said he'll call to see us soon. He also mentioned a window when the Government might allow people to move house because it's causing a log-jam in the property market. Perhaps we should call the solicitors sooner rather than later. As soon as this so-called window is announced there will be a rush to book removal men like never before.'

The next morning Millie got up early as usual, made tea and took it back to bed. She plugged her headphones in so as not to wake anyone else and started to listen to Georgey, her favourite presenter.

'Morning everyone. News just in, the Government has just announced that that there will be a relaxation of the house-moving rules for fourteen days from the 10th of December until Christmas Eve, so Mark in Scarbados, you've got your work cut out if you haven't started packing already.'

Crikey, thought Millie. That Mr James had better turn up soon. And where are we with the completion date? Talk about so many pieces in a jig-saw. She needn't have worried. Mr Hymer was on the ball already. He and his staff would be working flat out to secure more completions over the next month than in the whole of the year so far. In fact he was on the phone shortly after eight-thirty.

'I bring you all good news. Assuming there are no complications we are going to complete two days before Christmas Eve. Can I suggest that you book your removals firm without delay?'

13.

This was the news they had all been waiting for. All of a sudden, after so many delays and false starts, they were literally on the move. Reality started to sink in. This was no time for sentiment. It was 'all hands to the pumps' as Peter emphasised.

'Trust you to say that Dad' chirped Lucy over the breakfast table. 'We'll be proceeding north soon on a course of zero-zero-five at forty knots soon will we?'

'Don't be cheeky young lady. It's just dawned on me that you'll be sixteen soon and you can smoke and be a naughty girl ...'

'Dad! And you talk about me being cheeky!'

'Listen, Lucy, there'll be all sorts of temptations in Scarborough. You've all led a sheltered life on a nice housing estate with nice neighbours. There'll be all sorts of temptations on the coast.'

'Yeah like what? Ice-cream parlours and waffle bars? Come off it Dad.'

'Yes, there's all that as well but there's night life too in the town centre no doubt. And when you're eighteen you'll be able to ...'

This time it was the youngest daughter's turn to glare at him.

Mandy came into the room with several sheets of A4 white paper in her hand.

'Right, I've made a list of what we need to take on the day we move. Take a look please and see if you can add to the list. She passed it over to Pete who then started hunting for his reading glasses. He found them under yesterday's Hull Daily Mail the headline of which read – 'PM announces Xmas Holiday break from restrictions.' Maybe he had a heart after all. Maybe.

'Mandy, you've put Jamie's motor bike on the list.'

'But he hasn't passed his Test yet. And he won't be able to until they start again after the Covid epidemic is over.'

'He's got 'L' plates hasn't he? He can ride it to Scarborough. Surely?'

'Not at this time of year. The weather can be tricky at the best of times. No, I'm not having it. The bike will have to go in the removals van with everything else.'

The Viking alpha-female had spoken. The list was seemingly quite short but with the Wendover's sale including all fixtures and fittings they didn't have to worry about things like beds, linen and kitchen equipment.

'You know, Pete, we can get by with a minimum of stuff really can't we? And we haven't even decided yet if we're going to sell or keep this house. It can look after itself over the winter can't it? And if the weather gets really icy then the boiler thermostat will cut in. Pete, are you listening to me or what?'

'Sorry love, yes and of course if we need to pop back for anything the it's only just over an hour in the car. No holiday traffic at this time of year.'

Pete's mobile phone did a double-ping. It was Clayton James, the removal man texting:

I'll be with you at five-thirty sharp today. Check your loft and garage please. Most folks forget. Clayton.

'Oh heck, Pete. That hadn't even occurred to me, had it you?'

'To be honest, no love. We're not exactly used to moving are we?'

'Well, we've been here since just before Millie arrived. The move from our first little house on Holderness Road was traumatic enough and looking back we hardly owned a lot then did we? I think we moved here with one double bed, a twin-tub washer, a TV that was as deep as it was wide and that old Lec fridge that me Mam gave us! Bless her. I wish she could see us all now with two more grand-kids that she never saw. I'm coming over all weepy.'

'Come on, love. Lets have another look at that list then I'll check what's in the garage – Jamie's little Honda for a start! He won't want that leaving behind to collect in the Spring. He'll be wanting to explore Scarborough as soon as he can.'

'You mean Scarbados!'

The day passed quickly as they started to separate stuff into 'Take' or 'Leave' lists. Maybe they should have taken some more photographs when they had looked around the Wendover Hotel.

'Pete, can you remember if there was a desk in the hallway at the Wendover or not?'

'Search me, ask Millie.'

'She's out with Seb – its her turn. Come to think of it didn't she say she made two thirty second videos on her iPhone – upstairs and downstairs.'

'Can't we check the one on the Agent's website?'

'No we can't. As it's now sold 'subject to contract' the agent has taken it down. We'll just have to wait until Millie gets back. When she does, ask her to play us the video, or better still get her to send it to your iPhone. She'll know how to do it. I'm no good with these new-fangled gadgets. Give me a proper phone that's fixed onto a wall any day. And speaking of phones, has the Wendover got a land-line or not?'

'I think it did have but it's disconnected anyway. I cheekily tried it when we walked round and it was dead – not even a little humming noise. Come to think of it the phone was perched atop a wooden packing case in the hall, so I don't think there could have been a desk. Anyway, we'll see what Millie's video reveals. That sounds like Seb's bark outside. She wasn't long was she?'

'Well, it's dark already now the clocks have gone back.'

'Pass me your phone, Dad, then I'll transfer the two videos across. I'll do it now and just check that's they've arrived in your WhatsApp inbox.'

There were lots of pictures in Pete's inbox. Mostly they were of colleagues from the Pride of Bruges and friends in Belgium. She could tell that by the foreign beer labels on the bar tops and tables. It was good that he would be able to look back and reminisce despite the fact that a new life beckoned.

At precisely twenty-nine minutes past five a white Transit van pulled up outside the front window. Mandy spotted it first.

'There he is now – look. Bang on time. That augurs well for the day we move. I'll let him in. Pete, pop the kettle on there's a love. The least we can can do is give him a cuppa before he sets off home.

Mr Clayton James almost filled the entire door frame when he came in. Six foot two, if an inch, and almost as broad. Had Mandy been a New York cop she'd be shouting into her radio 'Caucasian, six-two, two hundred twenny pounds' but she wasn't. She was a Hull housewife from Holderness Road.

'Hello Mr James, come in – let me take your coat. Nasty out there now isn't it and dark. I hate winter nights do you?'

'Thank you Mrs Fishburn. I'm like you. Dark nights are no good for us. Delivering in daylight can be hard enough but with all these restrictions its even worse but we'll come to that later. Now, did I hear someone mention tea? Milk, no sugar please and as strong as it comes.' Straight to the point, that's Clayton.

'Shall we start upstairs. I've got my notebook and pen. I usually record notes on my phone but the last time I did that I accidentally erased it. I'm not too hot with this modern larky.'

'Then you have a lot in common with my husband Mr James, a lot.'

He walked into each bedroom in turn.

'So all the beds are staying here I take it? That doesn't leave a lot does it? Wardrobes?'

'They're staying too – most of them are modern fitted ones anyway. The contents will be going though. This is Millie's room, my eldest.' She opened the sliding, mirrored doors.'

'Jesus! How many dresses and trousers has she got? Enough to fill several charity shops by the look of it. And as for shoes! Is her middle name Imelda? Only joking. Right, next room please.'

Clayton took copious and accurate notes before they moved downstairs. Mugs of tea were waiting and they all 'took five' in the living room. But even when seated and having his toes sniffed by the suspicious Seb, he was still looking around and taking notes.

'Now, what about this large pictures on the wall? In the Navy were you, Mr Fishburn?'

He pointed to several acrylic paintings of various ferries that had plied between Hull and the Continent over the last two decades. He recognised one of them that had been out of service for over twenty years. That's the old Norland isn't it? A mate of mine had a son who was serving on it when it got taken over by the Admiralty to take troops to the Falklands War. A rum do that was. Anyway, are these your two girls?' Millie and Lucy had both just walked into the room.

'Yes this is Millie, my eldest, and this is Lucy.'

'Hi girls. OK look, you both seem to have enormous quantities of clothes and shoes, you particularly, Millie. Normally I would say take this opportunity to give away a lot of it to deserving charity shops before you move. Sadly, because of Covid, they're not currently accepting donations because of the risk of spreading the virus. Bonkers if you ask me but we are where we are.'

Both girls looked pleadingly at him, fervently hoping he wasn't going to suggest the tip. Clayton winked at Pete before his next line.

'So, I think the best course of action is to take half of what you've got to the public incinerator in Percival Street here in Hull and …' He didn't finish and Pete suddenly laughed out loud.

'Don't worry, girls, he's only joking but how many times have your mother and I told you to have a clear-out of your things? Anyway, Clayton. What's the verdict?'

'We're nowhere near finished my friend. What's in't garage? Let's go and take a look please? They went outside and with coats still inside it was distinctly chilly. Pete lifted the roller-door and switched on the strip light which soon flickered to life.

'Crikey, you didn't mention a motor bike even if it's only a small one. Them set of ladders are they to go as well? You'll be doing your own window cleaning for a while with all this Covid lark. And you know what Scarborough seagulls are like, or don't you? Messy blighters and so noisy too. And them step-ladders. Now, owt in't shed? Let's take a look. Mower eh? Well we can take it with the rest of the stuff or you can wait until the Spring and put it in the back of your estate. 'Owt in't conservatory? Let's take a look and I'll measure the furniture up, Most of that wicker-ware stuff just doesn't fold or dismantle easily. Now where's my measuring tape? Put the light on please.'

Pete did exactly that and instantly realised they had overlooked a major consideration – the palm trees and yucca plants.

'You're not telling me they're going as well? Really? Thems almost three metres I reckon. I'll check. Not quite, but it totally rules out using the smaller of my two vans. We'll need the twenty foot pantechnicon and even then it's gonna be tight. They'll have to lie flat and those pots will all have to be properly sealed. We don't want soil all overt van every time we go over a bump. Right, let's go back inside. Any chance of another cuppa while I work out a quote for you?'

Clayton switched his mobile phone to calculator mode and started pressing buttons. Even using the pantechnicon it was going to be tight. Click, click, click.

'Right, I play with a straight bat and I only ever give one quote. My total fee to move everything we've covered from here to Scarborough on the appointed date is nine hundred and ninety five pounds. Cash or a pre-cleared cheque or direct bank transfer into my account on the day.'

'Done, said Peter and they shook hands on it. Pete felt like he was shaking hands with a grizzly bear.

'I'll confirm everything in writing, including what you have to do to make it a smooth move for all of you. That includes you too young ladies. It's always an emotional time is moving home. Right, I'll be off. Thanks for the tea. I'll be dropping off plenty of flat-pack packing cases for you in a couple of days. Twenty cases each for the girls I think.' He winked at Pete again and with that he was gone.

Mandy reacted first. 'Well girls, you'd better get started tomorrow. You particularly, Imelda! Just how many pairs of shoes have you got? And do you ever wear even half of them?

14.

Two days later the same white van pulled up outside the Fishburn's house in Noseley Way. This time a tall youth about twenty jumped out of the cab and walked round to the back of the vehicle. He undid the bolt of the metal roller-door and, in an obviously practised motion, grabbed a handle and zoomed it skywards with a metallic, shrill, ring. He jumped into the back and seconds later threw what looked like half a ton of packaged flat-pack cardboard onto the kerbside. Mandy had already come to the front door.

'Morning, Mrs Fishburn. I'm Jack, Clayton's son. Dad says there are fifty flat-pack boxes here. I'll just snip the fasteners and then you can take them in a few at a time. I know they don't look like boxes right now but …'

'Oh that's fine, thanks. Pete's quite good at that sort of thing.' Actually he wasn't – as they discovered later that day. On the Pride of Bruges he was used to unpacking cases, not the other way round..

'Have you got time for a cuppa? If you're like your Dad you'll like your tea.'

'Thank you but no thank you. Oh, before I forget, here's our letter confirming all the arrangements. Please pay particular attention to the times involved. He's a stickler for timekeeping.'

'Yes, I had noticed. Thank you. The three point turn at the end of the road brought nosey neighbours to front windows. Maybe it should be called Nosey Way.

Yet again Mandy took a small kitchen knife to a white envelope. She was getting good at this.

Dear Mr & Mrs Fishburn

I write to confirm arrangements for your move from Kingswood, Hull to the Wendover Hotel, Scarborough on Friday the 20th December.

As agreed the price will be nine hundred and ninety five pounds – by cash or bank transfer to the details below. If paying by cheque please allow five days for the cheque to clear PRIOR to the removal date.

I have supplied you with fifty flat-pack boxes which I hope will prove sufficient. These are all 'one metre cube' boxes and understand that my loading calculations are precise. There is not a lot of room for leeway. To comply with safety rules, not to mention my insurers, the petrol tank of the Honda motorcycle must be drained prior to loading.

Kindly ensure that all cases and boxes are securely fastened with the special duct tape provided and that fragile articles are packed in the bubble-wrap, also provided. The other white tape is labelled FRAGILE in red and must be clearly visible on boxes containing glassware and such.

I am assuming that all five of you, and your lovely doggie, will be travelling in your own car. Can I suggest that you set off a short while before we do. Your earlier arrival time will allow you to fully open the doors, front and rear, of the Wendover to allow speedy access. Also, please check with the agents that they are either on site when you arrive or have made suitable arrangements for the handover of keys. Past experiences tell me that this seemingly simple procedure can end in misunderstandings the consequences of which you would not believe.

We will be attending your house at twelve noon sharp. I am allowing exactly an hour to pack the van, two hours travel time to be absolutely safe, and an hour to unload at the other end. In other words we should finish the job just as the light is gone. After all it is almost the Winter Solstice isn't it?

You have fourteen days to plan a hassle free move but please call me if you have any questions or misgivings about the proposed arrangements.

Yours

Clayton James

Mandy read the letter out loud to everybody, everybody that is except Jamie whose turn it was to take Seb out for "walkies."

'Well I must say, that seems very thorough doesn't it? And you can tell he's such a nice man. Did you hear that girls? Fourteen days! How are you getting on with sorting all your vast collection of clothes? We'll start by allocating you, say, four boxes each shall we? I suspect that Jamie will only need a couple – he's not like you two. Just as well I didn't have three girls. Tell you what, let's have a dummy run with one of these boxes and how to assemble them shall we? Pete, love, show us all how it's done will you?'

Pete was just about to start watching his favourite quiz show on TV, Pointless, and was not best pleased at having to perform a cross between Origami and assembling a purchase from IKEA.

'Oh all-right then if I must. Let's bring one of those boxes onto the lounge floor. Pass me that basic duct tape and the sharpest pair of scissors from the kitchen draw.'

It wasn't as easy as he'd thought. 'Fold side A first. Then side B. Then the two longest sides C and D over A and B, Holding the box carefully now invert it onto a flat surface like a level floor. After packing the goods safely then repeat the process with sides E,F,G and H. Apply sufficient tape to secure G & H which should then be secured with the tape from side to side and corner to corner like a Union Jack.

'OK, lets try it with something that doesn't weigh too much to test it first. Pass me all eight cushions in this room please.' A minute later and the national flag appeared in rude form.

Right, girls pick it up taking a side each. The box is quite big isn't it? We must be careful not to overload them. Lift!'

Two seconds later and all eight cushions were on the floor. They hadn't taped up C & D before inverting the box. They all laughed except Pete.

'Oh well, Dad, at least we know now how not to do it!'

Pete knew it wasn't his day and reached for the TV remote. He'd already missed the first ten minutes of Pointless. This whole escapade reminded him very much of an old TV show called The Generation Game where competing families are asked to perform tricky tasks against a ticking clock. Bruce Forsyth's catch phrases of 'Good game, good game' and 'Didn't he do well?!' echoed through his brain like an ear worm all evening. And there were still forty-nine more boxes to go. Roll on the 20th of the month when it would all be over.

15.

To describe the next fourteen days as frenetic was a gross understatement. Umpteen trips were undertaken to the public tips but even there long queues were to be found as scores of other families found themselves in a similar predicament. One estimate said that half a million households all over the country were going to move house in the fourteen day window. No wonder all the removal companies were booked up including Clayton James who was actually moving three families on the twentieth, the last official day.

The great day finally arrived and the Fishburn family were prepared as much as they could be. Millie and Lucy had needed six boxes each just for their clothes. As expected, Jamie managed quite adequately with only two – one for all his clothes and the other for his personal possessions which included framed photos of former Hull City teams and individual, autographed pictures of some of the star players in recent years. They were his crown jewels and to protect them he used more than his allocated share of bubble-wrap and the cosseted 'fragile' red and white tape. Before breakfast and while it was still dark Jamie had got his two boxes downstairs and into the garage for easy loading into the truck when it arrived. He put them next to his motorbike so that all his stuff could be loaded at the same time and unloaded together at the other end. He had rather fancied arriving in his new town on a motorbike like a latter day Steve McQueen but on reflection his mother was right to veto his idea. The weather forecasts for Hull and Scarborough differed markedly for the day ahead. Jamie had already added 'Scarborough' to the weather App on his cellphone to accompany Hull and had seen that whilst Hull was set cool but fair for the day, Scarborough looked decidedly "squiffy" with an easterly Force Four wind backing northerly. His father Peter had schooled him on meteorological matters since he was a nipper and the ship's barometer that had been on the bulkhead of his father's cabin on the Pride of Bruges for years would now take 'Pride of Place' on his bedroom wall at the Wendover. It was a top of the range example by the London company Comitti & Sons and mounted on a plaque of the finest hand-polished mahogany. The engraving on the brass tag was minimal and simply read 'To Peter. SVG'. Perhaps it had been given to him by the ship's Master after ten years service on the vessel.

In contrast, the preparation for departure by both his sisters was on the verge of disastrous. Millie was mad with Lucy for grabbing on extra box to add to her allocated six.

'Why have you got an extra one? That's not fair.'

'It's not just for me! I've put all Seb's stuff in there. Both his baskets, his favourite rugs, bowls and his 'Reserved for Dog' cushion that I bought him for his birthday.'

'That's ridiculous. He was a rescue dog so we don't even know his real birthday. The vet said he was probably about …'

'His birthday is the day we adopted him – August 1st – Yorkshire Day two years ago.'

''So if the vet said he was about two years old that makes him four but you treat him like he's a baby not a young adult dog.'

'He's my dog not yours?' Mum suddenly arrived on the scene.

'Stop arguing you two. It's eleven o'clock and I'm making a final brew before we pack up the last of the kitchen stuff into that box over there. It'll be nigh on five o'clock before we can brew-up at the other end.'

'Mam, what are we going to eat tonight anyway? There's nothing at the other end is there? In fact those fridges and freezers probably aren't even switched on yet.'

Mandy tried not to look shocked. She had completely overlooked that fact. She had remembered to pack two flasks of chilled milk and a 'family pack' of two hundred Yorkshire tea bags but food? Oh dear what an oversight but there had been so many things to remember and think about. Thinking on her feet and out loud she came up with a solution.

'If we go into Scarborough by the same route as last time we go past that LIDLs don't we? We'll stop there quickly and get enough food to last us a day or two. There were two microwaves in the Wendover's kitchen if I recall so we won't starve. Anyway, look sharp it's gone eleven-thirty and Mr James is never late.'

She was right there. In fact he was twenty minutes early. The sky, dim as it already was, almost disappeared as the giant truck inched slowly in reverse and onto the drive, leaving just a minimum of space to work in between the vehicle and the garage door which was open. The view inside was now just boxes, boxes and even more boxes. At the far end Jamie's Honda was totally invisible.

Clayton jumped out of the cab seemingly wearing only a thin long-sleeved green sweatshirt with the firm's 'CJ' logo embossed on it.

'Goodness you'll be cold Mr James. I'd make you some hot tea but we've just packed the kettle and mugs into the last box.'

'Morning, not a bad day for it. I don't feel the cold and by the time all your stuff's in't truck I'll be well hot, trust me.' He barked orders at the two young lads, one of which was his son who had dropped off the packing boxes exactly two weeks earlier.

'Get that cardboard down from the drive right into the house and into the conservatory. I don't want any mess off yer shoes in't house. Jump to it! Right we'll start with all those bloody trees. We'll take them out through the conservatory at the back and then down the side. I said jump to it!'

Amazingly, in just under an hour, they were good to go. All fifty boxes, a motorbike and half of Kew Gardens were safely secured in the truck.

Windows and doors were secured and a final check made of each room to make sure nothing vital had been left behind.

'All clear. We are Go for Launch!' shouted Pete who just for a second thought he was the Range Officer at Cape Canaveral. They were all in the car and Seb took up his usual station right in the back. He barked profusely as they left Noseley Way for the last time as a family. He knew something was going on.

'Well Pete, so much for us leaving before the truck. What's the plan now?'

'Well Clayton said to go 'over the top' via Driffield which will be a bit shorter route and quicker than his route up the coast road. I suspect they'll stop at that mobile transport caff in that lay-by just this side of Brid for bacon butties and teas. Jack was saying that they'd already done two shorter moves in the Brid area before they came to us. They'll be starving now.'

They got out of greater Hull and onto the road to Beverley, the lovely county town of East Yorkshire. Millie and Pete both grinned as they passed the garden centre where they had obtained the palms and yuccas. The imposing superstructure of Beverley Minster appeared in the distant gloom of a sky that seemed to be darkening the further north they travelled. Twenty minutes later and they got onto the Driffield by-pass and past the show ground which hosted the country's biggest one-day agricultural show in July every year. That is every year except this one. Covid had affected everything and everyone. Inexplicably, the traffic started to slow as they approached the turn-off for Scarborough and RAF Staxton Wold. A Humberside Police vehicle was parked on the kerbside with its blue lights flashing. It brought back nasty memories of the time the same Force had ordered them to 'go home' when attempting a visit to Hornsea months earlier. A uniformed Officer came to the window.'

'What's your intended destination, Sir.'

'Scarborough, officer. We're moving house today. It's the last day we can under the temporary relaxation of the rules and ..'

'That's fine, Sir, but the reason for stopping all vehicles right now is to advise you of adverse weather conditions. Sudden snow squalls that weren't forecast have made the road north of Langtoft almost impassable. Only RAF personnel in 4 x 4 vehicles are being allowed through until further notice. But don't worry the coast road is reported as clear, so far anyway. Take the second exit and follow the signs to Nafferton and Bridlington. Safe journey, Sir.'

He walked on to the next car in the line, its exhaust throwing visible hot air into the air which seemed to be getting colder by the minute. Ten miles east, the removal guys were indeed consuming bacon butties and steaming mugs of tea.

'More tea, lads? There's no hurry. We're well ahead of time. They'll be there in the next half-hour opening the doors and putting all the lights on.' Had he had a nautical background, like Pete, he would have noticed a darkening sky and a change in wind direction from the north.

16.

'That's the third time I've seen the same sign for Nafferton, I'm sure. Are you certain we're on the right road? The police officer said …'

'No I'm not, to be honest.' Pete's voice was more than a little strained.'We should have seen a sign for Bridlington by now or a place called Carnaby.'

'Let's stop and set the satnav to the Wendover's address and postcode shall we?' Lucy interrupted them.

'Yes, good idea. Seb's getting agitated. I think he wants a wee.' Dad agreed.

'Right that settles it then. There's a lay-by up head four hundred yards. And please don't tell me you saw the sign for it ten minutes ago.'

Lucy got out the car and affixed a chain to Seb's collar. The last thing anybody wanted right now was for him to dash across the road in search of new smells. Not there was any traffic to worry about. Pete got out to stretch his legs for a minute and glanced skywards. It was a really dirty grey and almost on cue he noticed a few snow flakes fluttering down.

'Oh my God, that's all we need. Come on Seb, come on Lucy. Jump in. Let's be off.'

The newly programmed TomTom started its job immediately and the silky smooth female voice gave her orders:

'At the next roundabout, take the second exit.'

'So that's where we went wrong! We have been here before and we took the third exit. I think we've been right round Nafferton twice. Does it have a ring-road?'

'Mandy, I don't know and right now I don't care to be honest. Twenty two miles to go according to the satnav. Oh heck, it's a proper snow shower now. Even so we should make it within about forty-five minutes.'

Seventy-five minutes later and they were on the outskirts of Scarborough and a welcoming sign read 'Scarborough Town Centre one mile' but the top few inches of the green paint was already trimmed with snow that had frozen. Then Pete had an awful thought.

'Just realised, because of the diversion we won't be coming into town via that LIDLs store will we? Keep your eyes skinned for an alternative, all of you.'

Millie was first to spot a possible solution.

'There look! Ahead on the right! Looks like a Sainsbury's Express or whatever they call them these days. Pull in on the left. It looks like it's still open. There's lights on.'

Two minutes later and Millie and her mother were inside the shop. They were the only customers. The sole checkout girl spoke out.

'You're lucky. We're just about to close early because of the weather. Awful isn't it?'

'Believe it or we're just in the process of moving today. It was quite fine when we left Hull but it's terrible here. We need some foodstuffs to last us a few days. You know easy microwavable ready meals – that kinda thing.'

'The chilled cabinets and freezers are over there, love. Not a right lot to choose from sorry to say. Lots of flats and bedsits round 'ere and folks have been stocking up. I can't see us getting any more deliveries now until after Christmas.

I hope it's not going to be like that Beast from the East like what we had a few years ago. Any help just shout.'

The phrase was lost on Millie and Mandy. Ten minutes later and five vegetarian lasagnes, five sweet and sour chicken (Chinese style) with rice meals, five boxes of vegetarian spring rolls and three tins of chicken chunks in a white wine sauce were squeezed into the back with Seb.'

'Right according to TOM we are only two miles from the Wendover.'

The rest of the journey was plain sailing by comparison. As they past Peasholm Park on the left a large white truck heading in the opposite direction left a maelstrom of dirty sleet across their windscreen.

'They must be in a hurry. Hey-up I think we're almost there. I know where we are now. Hooray!'

'You have arrived at your destination.' Thank God for technology. But several surprises awaited them.

Every single light in the Wendover Hotel seemed to be switched on. The outer front door appeared slightly ajar and there were two strangers in the lounge window. There was a criss-cross of large tyre markings impressed in the two inches of snow in the road outside and two perfectly straight parallel tracks on the hotel's drive. There were dozens of footprints some of them obliterated by snowfall. The front door opened wide and a late middle aged chap came out and half walked, half slithered to the window of their car. He looked frozen and he'd only been outside for seconds. Pete wound down the window before he'd even turned the engine off. The chap seemed friendly enough but who the heck was he?

'Good afternoon, or should I say evening? You'll be Mr Fishburn I assume and family?' He peered through the window at the Frozen Five plus one dog.

'Yes. Are you from the Agents – Hopper and Co.?'

'No. My name's Garry, Garry Ritson and that's my wife Shirley in the foyer. It's been a right carry-on. Like one of them Carry On films. That Mr Hopper came and knocked on our door this morning about elevenish. He looked awful and was wearing a blue Covid mask. Said he'd tested positive this morning. He was profusely apologetic but asked us if we could take care of this bunch of keys until you arrived. There's that many of them I feel like a prison officer at Armley. He said to expect you about two hours ago.'

'Bad weather and bad planning to be honest. I hope the removal people aren't going to be long …'

'What? You've just missed them by about five minutes my friend. I've never seen three men work so fast in my life. All your stuff is safely inside. Fifty large cardboard boxes, tons of other stuff, a motorbike which is in the shed out back and, how could I forget, a veritable tropical garden. They're all in the conservatory.'

'How kind of you. And sorry, where did you say you live?'

'Next door, forty feet away. It's the only property on this road that hasn't been converted to a B & B or a hotel – not quite big enough really. Anyway let's help you in. Oh what a lovely doggie!'

'That's Seb, our labradoodle, Mr Ritson. Do you mind taking hold of his lead while I get out. He's been here before when we looked round the place months ago.'

'Isn't he lovely? We've got three dogs of our own – all little Yorkies. You'll have to meet them when you've got unpacked.'

'Oh I'd love to, thank you.' Lucy had made her first friend in Scarborough within a minute of arriving. Pete took charge. Somebody had to.

'Right you lot, let's get inside. Chop-chop.'

Mrs Ritson was just as homely as she looked. Seventy-ish with still almost black hair tied back.'

'We've done what we can for you – once we'd mastered all the keys that is. The boiler has been switched on and every room downstairs at least seems warm. We turned on the two radiators in the conservatory as soon as the removal man put all those trees in there. I thought I was seeing things!'

'That is so thoughtful of you. Thank you.'

'Oh yes and we switched the fridges and freezers on for you too. They're chilling nicely. Mind you the place was already cold until we turned the heating on. He's left a card and bottle of something in the kitchen. What a nice man. He left me his business card. We'll book him when we eventually downsize, won't we Garry? I said won't we Garry?' But Garry was already back in his own house next door. Women could talk forever couldn't they?'

The card said 'Welcome to your new home. Have a drink on us. It was a litre bottle of Prosecco. Five glasses were quickly found from behind the compact Bar in the dining room. Mandy did the honours and filled all five glasses to the brim.

'Cheers everyone and welcome to our new home in Scarborough!'

'I think you mean Scarbados, Mum!' retorted Millie.

They all cried. Even Seb looked a little teary. He couldn't wait to get back into that garden and have his second wee in Scarbados.

17.

Driiinnng! Driiinnng!

The front doorbell of the Wendover Hotel was ringing for the first time in many months. It sounded like it was hesitant and out of practice. Lucy was nearest the door and eventually managed to open it. Well half of it anyway. It was one of those heavy, double-doors that met in the middle. Outside was Shirley Ritson in the gloom of the early morning and it was barely light.'

'Hello, Lucy, and good morning everyone. I thought this might help on your first morning here. You won't have managed to unpack much yet I'm sure.'

On a large plastic tray that depicted a typical seaside scene of boats, a lighthouse and a sandy beach was a selection of warm bread rolls, toast and croissants – all covered in a check tea towel to keep them as warm as possible for as long as possible. A butter dish and a small pot each of jam and marmalade accompanied this veritable dawn feast. Mandy shouted down from the first floor landing.

'Lucy, who on Earth is it for goodness sake? And at this time! It's hardly light.'

'It's Shirley from next door and look what she's brought us – breakfast!'

Mandy was soon downstairs, albeit in a dressing gown and slippers.

'Oh Shirley, that is so kind of you! We didn't fancy vegetarian spring rolls for breakfast. Thank you so much. Pete! Come down and see what Shirley's brought us.'

Three minutes later and there were six bodies around the kitchen table with six steaming mugs of Yorkshire Tea.

'We haven't unpacked the box with the family sized toaster in yet. And even if we had we've no bread, butter or anything. That snow-storm put paid to all our good intentions yesterday. Where are the nearest shops by the way? We still haven't found our bearings yet.'

'Go downhill to the junction and turn right, then left just past the theatre entrance. A hundred yards past that is one of those convenience stores that sells everything from bread to beer and milk to magazines. You know the sort. Because it sells food it's been exempted from all those recent restrictions.'

'Gosh, that's fortunate. Are you sure it'll be open?'

'Oh yes, Above the store is a block of posh new apartments and many of them are let out to folks for a week at a time, or even just a few days. With restrictions lifting for a while I bet they're nearly all booked up.' Jamie had already gobbled up a croissant and two slices of toast.

''Mum, I'll get the bike out of the shed and go and buy a few essentials shall I? Just until we can do a proper shopping expedition in the car.'

'That's a great idea. And be careful. It still looks slippery out there and wet slush is awful. Where's your helmet?'

'I packed that separately in one of my two boxes. Unlike my sisters I'm organised!

He spoke too soon. Five minutes later he came in the back door looking furious.

'I don't believe it. It just won't start.' Shirley looked a little guilty.

'Oh heck, sorry, we meant to pass a message on to you from the removal man. He said to tell you that they had to empty its petrol tank before leaving Hull and that he had stipulated that in his instructions.

'What? Well that's news to me! Nobody told me. Well that's that then. We'll have to take the car, Dad. Best make a list, Mam, and do the job properly. And don't forget we want a small frozen turkey – about four kilos – and all the bits and bobs that go with it. You know stuffing, sprouts, cranberries – the full Monty.'

Twenty minutes later and the family car was parked on double yellow lines right outside the store with the large tailgate open and pointing towards the sky which had brightened considerably.

'We won't get done for parking as we're loading aren't we? Lets go in.' They grabbed two shopping baskets each. It was a long list.

'Right where shall we start, Jamie? Let's start on the left where the bread is and work our way clockwise around to the frozen section before we hit the checkouts.'

They were in for a shock at the frozen poultry cabinet. It was in darkness and switched off. Just a few feet away the sole checkout girl saw their anguish.

'You'll be lucky, sorry love. What was it you wanted?'

'A small bronze turkey about four kilos please.'

'Where have you been for the last two weeks? Not seen hide nor hair of any kind of turkey, chicken or goose for yonks. You can blame Covid. No poultry deliveries for weeks, love. I bet there isn't a turkey left in Scarborough.'

Brenda, Team Leader, from her company badge, rang all the purchases through the electronic till at the speed of light and offered them four 'eco-friendly bags for life' as the current jargon had it. Pete paid with contact-less plastic and at least the reassuring 'ping' announced a successful purchase – minus the festive buzzard of course. They loaded the four bags into the back, jumped in and Pete started the engine.

'Shall we have a spin round the Drive before we get back? There's nothing we've bought that's going to spoil or melt is there?'

'No, not in these temperatures, Dad. Sure, why not. The girls will be ages unpacking. We're better off out the way. Which way do we go?'

'Jamie, there's only one way – down to the roundabout then right. Come on. Looks like the tide's right in. Look at those waves splashing over the sea wall. Wow! That car over there just copped it. It's sea-water too. Salt's very bad for cars. Let's do a U-turn and go back home OK?'

'Agreed. Home it is.'

It was the first time either of them had referred to the Wendover Hotel as 'home.' They had been out for less than half an hour but the downstairs rooms were already in a state of chaos. It looked like all but a handful of the fifty boxes had been slit open with their contents spewing out over almost every square foot of floor. The girls were arguing.

'How come half of my jumpers are in your boxes? No wonder I can't find anything.'

Millie was not best pleased with her younger sibling.

''You can't talk. How come I've got Seb's favourite cushion in my Box No. 6? I can't find my favourite Levis either – the ones with the designer holes in.'

'It's cold enough already without 'Holy Jeans' – it's colder than 'Ull.'

'Just stop it you two. And when a box is emptied revert it to being flat and we'll store them in the garage for now until they can all be re-cycled. What does everyone want for lunch? I thought maybe soup and sandwiches. I've found some tins of chicken soup and Ox Tail soup in one of the boxes I packed a week ago. And tins of spam and corned beef. We won't starve. So chaps, leave the turkey out in the pantry where it can defrost slowly in time for Christmas Day.'

'It's bad news love, I'm afraid. Apparently there aren't any in town and there hasn't been for many days. Any ideas?' Everybody looked aghast. That is everybody except Lucy who didn't even try to suppress a smile.

'Good! That'll teach you. I'm going vegetarian. I was going to start on the first of January as a New Year's resolution. But in the circumstances I think I'll start right now. Chicken or Ox-tail soup did you say? No thank you! Got any tomato or lentil?'

She wasn't joking either. Her flaming red pony tail confirmed she was a fully paid-up, if junior, Viking from the same mould as her mother. Millie was quite placid, like her father. How would their personalities change or develop as they acclimatised to their new surroundings?

By mid-afternoon Pete had rigged up the family's wide screen HD television that had been wrapped up by Clayton James with so much bubble-wrap it looked like a giant prehistoric insect cocooned and about to morph into something else.

'Well this is good news, it's working normally using the sockets to the main aerial on the roof. Uh-oh, what's this come up on the screen? New channels found, it says. What the heck do we do now?'

'Dad, you're useless at this. Pass me the remote please.' She pressed the OK button.

'There you are. Bye-bye Humberside and hello BBC Look North.' The News was just starting.

'Breaking news, the Government has just announced the Christmas break from Covid Rules will now be only forty-eight hours and not four days as previously announced.'

'Oh God, when will it ever end?' sighed Mandy. Just when? Pete partially retrieved the gloom and doom.

'Hey come on! Look on the bright side of life! Today is the shortest and darkest day, the Winter Solstice. If we were all Druids or Pagans we'd be out before dawn and welcoming the sunrise as a New Year starts. So let's mark today as the Hotel Scarbados' birthday. A new start for us all. Even you, Seb. Jamie, let's break out that bottle of Prosecco we got this morning with all those groceries.'

'That wasn't on my list, Pete. You crafty so and so. You didn't say.'

'I don't tell you everything, darling. Nearly everything but not everything.'

He could say that again.

18.

The next three days were spent doing the rest of the unpacking. It was some task. On Christmas Eve the last of the flat-pack boxes were once again restored to their original state and stored in the garage. Mandy made a mental note to call Clayton James in the New Year to see if he could use them again with another customer. That might be a better idea than recycling come to think of it. Just how many paper plates could they be turned into anyway?

The prospect of a Christmas without the traditional turkey was disappointing but they would try to make the most of it. They had however managed to buy a half a dozen of those small microwavable Christmas puddings and a half a bottle of brandy to pour over them with the festive blue flame. The only Christmas decoration would be one of those electric candle displays in the form of an inverted 'V' which they found in a cupboard. It was duly plugged in and placed in the Hall window facing the road. The sooner the world realised that the Hotel was occupied again the better.

They had just settled down in the main lounge to watch an old Christmas edition of Morecambe and Wise when the front doorbell rang for only the second time in months. It was the Ritsons from next door.

'Come in, come in! You look nithered. What's up, Shirley?'

'We've just had some awful news, haven't we Garry? Our daughter, son-in-law and granddaughter aren't coming for Christmas after all. It's so upsetting.'

Oh no. Don't tell me they've tested positive for …'

'No they're fine thank goodness. No, it's just the time frame of things. With the Government changing its mind on how long the so-called Christmas break can last, it's put the kibosh on all their plans. They were intending to drive back to Sheffield where they live on Boxing Day after lunch but it would now mean only being able to stay one night so they've abandoned the plan. They say they'll save the time off for Easter – whenever that is next year. We haven't even looked at the calendar yet to be fair.' The Fishburns could only sympathise.

'Oh dear me. Well if we'd been a bit more organised and Covid hadn't got in the way we'd have been more than happy to ask you to join us. Sadly we haven't even got a turkey let alone any Christmas crackers and …'

'That's why we've popped round. We have a large turkey which will do for the four of us for Christmas day with some left over for cold cuts on Boxing Day and home-made turkey curry for goodness knows how long so we'd be delighted if you'd all come and join us.'

'Five of you, you mean?'

'No, our granddaughter Chloe who's ten, decided months ago to become a vegetarian. We've got one of those awful nut roast things for her. I think I'll freeze it for when they do actually come over. Garry won't touch it and to be honest I'm not keen.'

Lucy had overheard the entire conversation and was beaming from ear to ear.

'We'd just love to come wouldn't me Mam?! And I'm a vegetarian now as well so if Chloe doesn't mind I'll eat her lunch?' Shirley and Garry were over the moon. They all were.

'Shall we say about one o'clock then? There'll be time for a little sherry first. We're not big drinkers but it is Christmas after all isn't it?'

All of a sudden the gloom lifted. They might not be having their first Christmas dinner in the Wendover but it would be so nice to meet their new neighbours properly. How kind and they had only been in town for three days.

'Dig out your Christmas jumpers everyone!' yelled Pete.

It was a minor miracle that everyone could find their festive clothes. They even found Seb's Christmas collar with velvet green and red holly. Everyone went to bed that night with a smile on their face. How would they feel on their first Christmas Day in Scarbados? Only time would tell.

Christmas mornings always seem to be terribly dark and this was no exception. Dawn hadn't even broken and Seb was barking at the back door leading into the garden indicating his wish for a pee. He was well-trained like that and Lucy went downstairs in a thick dressing gown and slippers to let him out. She went into the conservatory and threw the switch on a powerful two hundred watt LED light mounted on the rear wall of the hotel. It illuminated the entire garden instantly. Seb dutifully trotted the thirty yards down to the very end of the garden and cocked his leg in the same spot he always did. It was strange. Post pee, he had a good sniff around the tree that he now regarded as his own domain. It was an evergreen about twenty feet tall with a main trunk about eighteen inches round its circumference. Lucy thought it might have been a silver birch but trees weren't her scene. If it didn't bark or like "walkies" she wasn't interested. She opened the conservatory door to shout for Seb to come back in. He took not the blindest bit of notice. In fact he seemed to be digging!

'Seb! Seb! Seb! Come back inside now. Now!'

Eventually he must have tired of her shrill, nagging voice and trotted to the now wide-open conservatory door.

'Oh, Seb. Just look at you! Soil all over your nose and muddy front paws. Let me get an old towel. What on Earth did you think you were doing? Tunnelling to Australia?'

It would be many days before Lucy would come to realise just how close she had come to the truth. The rest of the household was starting to get up now. Mandy was in full flow.

'Right everyone, the kettles on, the coffee's on and it's scrambled eggs with smoked salmon for breakfast. We always had that for Christmas breakfast back in 'Ull and we're not changing any traditions just because we've moved fifty miles north. Some traditions must not be broken and this is one of them. Good God, have you seen Seb's face? He's covered in soil. Where's he been?'

'Sorry, Mam. I thought I'd cleaned him up. I'll finish him off properly.'

''I asked where's he been? He never got like that before we moved.'

'It's a bit weird, Mam. He's got this fascination with that tree at the bottom of the garden.'

'Which tree? There's a few.'

'The only one that's in leaf that's not a palm tree. It's right at the end, Remember the first time we came to have a look round? Well he made a bee line for it as soon as he got out the car. He does his business there on auto-pilot. And now he seems to be digging a hole. It's about six inches deep already.'

'Well I suppose we don't have to worry about poop bags for the time being but you'll have to start taking him for longer walkies soon. Perhaps after lunch you could ask Garry and Shirley where they take their "Yorkies for walkies" around here. Now then, who's going to help me serve up? Anyone, or shall I eat all the smoked salmon myself?'

By twelve forty-five they were all spruced up and good to go. Even Jamie had polished his smart black shoes. Since lockdown he'd only ever worn trainers – something he had in common with half the country. When it was over, please God, millions would have to learn how to dress properly and interact with their fellow man. It would take time. Only Lucy had reservations about going next door for lunch with the Ritsons.

'Mam, do you think they would mind if we brought Seb along with us.'

'I don't know, love, but it would be polite to ask first. Why don't you just pop next door and ask.'

Thirty seconds later and she was back.

'No problem! Their Yorkies are lovely – I just met them all. Candy, Shandy and Randy – he's the only boy and getting on a bit I'd say.'

'Probably nagged to death by the other two!' said Pete. 'Come on it's rude to be late. We'll leave some lights on. What's this switch here, the one on its own? 'Nothing seems to have come on does it. Perhaps it's on a timer of some kind. I'll leave it on anyway. You never know. I've got the keys. Let's go!'

The welcome could not have been warmer. A log fire was ablaze in the large lounge with the three Yorkies half asleep sprawled in parallel across the shag pile rug. Within seconds Candy and Shandy were springing up to Lucy's knees and she'd only met them minutes earlier. Randy just dozed on, oblivious to the rest of the world.

Garry came into the room with a silver tray bearing seven matching sherry schooners and a large unopened bottle of Croft's Original Pale Cream sherry.

'It was my mother's favourite and it's a little tradition on Christmas Day. Bless her.'

'We all have our family traditions at Christmas don't we' added Mandy. 'Ours is scrambled eggs with smoked salmon for breakfast.'

'Oh heck, well I hope you've left room for all this turkey. It's a twelve pounder, slightly bigger than we'd normally get but we were just grateful to get one at all. What with bird 'flu and Covid and everything else. We should all count our blessings. In fact I'll carve some for you to take home wih you for sandwiches shall I, Mandy?'

'I've got a better idea but I'll tell you after lunch. Now, can I give you a hand in the kitchen?'

The lunch was superb and a totally unexpected surprise from the corned beef hash they thought they would have to settle for twenty-four hours earlier. Half way through, Lucy felt the cold wet nose of a dog nuzzling her calf under the table. He must have smelt turkey – one of his favourites. She surreptitiously held a chunk of nut-roast under the tablecloth in his general direction. He sniffed it and turned away. A vegetarian dog Seb was not. He went back to the rug in the lounge and resumed his kip with his new canine pals. In any case his mind was still on that tree.

They had just about finished the main course when suddenly a flash of red light outside took them all completely by surprise. It seemed to flicker in the sky and then stay permanently in the air. Garry reacted first.

'Ah, don't worry. It's your neon Wendover Hotel sign at the front. It's light sensitive and with the dark afternoon it's just clicked on automatically. There's an over-ride switch somewhere that you might not have found yet, Pete.'

'Actually, I think I have found it already. At least I know what it is now. We'll be arranging to have it taken down soon and replaced with a new one.'

'What for? Don't you like it?'

'It's fine but we're going to change the name of the Hotel to ....'

'Have a guess!' shouted Millie. It was my idea.'

'I've no idea. Go on, do tell.'

'Hotel Scarbados!' A wry smile slowly spread across Garry's face.

'Oh wow, wow, wow! I love it, I love it! It seems to have become everyday slang in the last few years. You've only just moved here of course but if you tune in to BBC Radio York fairly early you'll hear ...'

'Garry, I do, and I've been listening to it for months, in fact ever since we decided to move here! It took a while to wean me off Viking Radio. You know what us Hull folk are like – loyal and strong willed!'

'Er yes, I'd noticed. What do you think, Shirley?'

'Well, its a bit too common-sounding for me but at least it sticks – unlike the name Wendover. Apparently the previous owners came from Manchester many years ago and brought the name with them. We never really had a lot to do with them. They made it quite obvious they didn't like dogs from the outset. Never the twain shall meet and all that.'

'What was it called before the Wendover?'

'No idea. It was before our time. We've only been here ten years! Ha! We bought it for our retirement really – by the sea and the parks – great for dogs! Now what was it you were going to say about the turkey leftovers, Mandy? You didn't finish what you were saying.'

19.

It had been another one of the Fishburn's family traditions since they had moved into Noseley Way all those years ago. Pete's Boxing Day 'bubble and squeak' was something else. He'd picked up the recipe from a chef on the Pride of Bruges in the early days and then tried it out on the family when not at sea. But it wasn't just the food that made Boxing Day so special. It was the big race at Kempton Park – the King George VI Stakes. After the traditional lunch of cold turkey with bubble and squeak followed by cheese and biscuits the whole family would gather round the TV to watch the big race. In the morning as soon as the bookies were open, Pete would drive to the nearest one and put a one pound 'to win bet' on every horse in the race, each one on a separate betting slip. Then, once home, he would roll them up like cigarette 'roll-ups' and put them in a wine glass. After lunch everyone would pick one out like a short straw and hope they had drawn the winner and preferably one with long odds. Just after ten o'clock they had to get to it. Jamie had picked the winner last year, Tornado Flyer, and he was keen to win again. Forty quid had been his lucky reward.

'Dad, I'll come into town with you. I've looked on Google Maps and found three bookmakers close to each other. One of them's bound to be open. Do we need to wear a mask do you think?'

'I've no idea, Jamie. The rules have become so complicated in recent weeks. Is Scarborough in the same Covid-Zone as Hull? Does it really matter any more anyway? By all accounts it's back to square one after tomorrow – 'You must stay at home' and all that nonsense from Downing Street. Anyway, let's be off and we've got some masks in the glove box if needs be. You can navigate.'

Ten minutes later and they were in the town centre at some traffic lights.

'Which way, Jamie?'

'Not sure Dad, but I can see a bookies up there look. There's people outside in a queue.'

'Oh well at least it's open. The lights are changing ... look there's a car park on the left. It's almost empty. Bingo! Let's park up and both go in together.' The security doorman was not exactly full of the Christmas spirit.

'Only six people allowed in the shop at the same time and masks on please.'

They complied and waited until what looked like a man and wife couple exited the shop.

'Right, you two. In you go.' They made a bee-line for a screen that gave the runners and riders for the race – the biggest one in the country on Boxing Day.

'How many runners are there, Dad? Is that ten?

'No, look. Two are non-runners so that's down to eight. Grab eight of those little betting slips. I'll write down the first four, you the last four. Eight pounds in total. A small price to pay for the amount of fun it will generate.'

They were home by eleven o'clock and hot coffee awaited them and they sat at the kitchen table rolling up the eight betting slips.

'Dad, I've just had a thought. There'll be seven of us and eight betting slips. What shall we do with the eighth one that's left in the glass?' Somebody had an instant solution – Lucy.

'That can be Seb's. If he wins then it will pay for lots of treats. Where is he anyway? He was here a few minutes ago.'

Thirty yards away, Seb was scratching and digging under his favourite tree. The progress he was making to the land Down Under was slow but still probably faster than the national HS2 project.

'Right, Pete, now you've done that you can make a start on that bubble and squeak of yours. You might as well show us all what's in it then we can do it all on our own.'

'No chance! In any case I prepared it all last night while you lot were watching Only Fools and Horses. All I need now is two big frying pans or skillets and extra virgin olive oil – lots of it!'

'That's not fair, Dad. It's a hundred per cent veggie isn't it? I want to be able to make it myself.'

'Oh all-right. Next time you can watch me. But not a word to the others about the ingredients OK?

'OK Dad, I promise. I might tell Seb though.'

She winked at her Dad and he winked back. Just after one o'clock and the Ritsons arrived with what looked like a half a Norfolk turkey all nicely carved and wrapped up in tinfoil. A half a jar of cranberry sauce, piccalilli and an unopened jar of silverskin pickled onions completed the offerings.

'Oh my, what a gorgeous smell coming from your kitchen. What is it?'

'That's Pete's secret bubble and squeak. He won't tell me what's in it. Let's go into the dining room shall we? The table is set for eight although there's only seven of us. It's another of our little quoibles and its a symbolic gesture for any hungry traveller who might drop in at the last minute.'

'How quaint. But what a lovely idea.'

Pete had found a traditional brass gong with a velvet-covered hammer in a cupboard and couldn't wait to use it properly for the first time. He felt like that chap who banged a huge gong at the start of all Rank movie productions.

'Gong! Gong! Luncheon is served, ladies and gentlemen. Please take your seats in the dining room.'

A half an hour later and they were all absolutely stuffed. Lucy was allowed a double helping of the bubble and squeak in lieu of turkey. She had eaten all of the Ritson's nut-roast the day before. Millie brought in warm mince pies and coffee and all was well with the world. There was still almost an hour to go before the big race on TV. Sadly it wouldn't have the same ambience as usual because the racing authorities had decided to run the race behind closed doors, so to speak, without the usual thousands of spectators gathered to watch the race made famous by the legendary Desert Orchid who had won it several times running. The tens of thousands of National Hunt followers attending the Cheltenham Festival at the start of the Covid outbreak had been blamed for causing a 'spike' in Covid cases. If the truth be told, nobody really knew, let alone the so-called experts who seemed to dictate to everybody every aspect of how they conducted their lives.

'OK everyone, let's pick out a betting slip each' chirped up Pete. 'This is how it works. Everybody take one and then unroll it to reveal the name of their horse.' They all did until there was just one left. 'That's Seb's' said Lucy.

Shortly after three o'clock the Starting Officer brought the horses and jockeys to a roughly straight line pulled the lever to lift the starting tape. They're off! The TV commentator did his very best to enliven the atmosphere in the absence of noise from a non-existent crowd. It was a long race, over three miles and many fences. With a furlong to go only two horses were left in the running with a realistic chance of running.

'And it's neck and neck between Scarlet Emperor and Givethedogabone. There's nothing in it. It's a photo-finish. We'll have to wait for the judges decision. It won't take long. Here it comes over the Tannoy now.'

'First, number three, Givethedogabone – second number eight, Scarlett Emperor – third …

They all looked down at their betting slips, crestfallen. No luck.

'Just a minute, what about the one left over. It must be Seb's horse. Open it.' Sure enough. It read Givethedogabone £1 win. How much has he won, Dad?'

'They'll give us the odds on-screen in a minute. Here it is 3-1 favourite. So he's won three quid plus his stake back – four quid.'

'Is that all? It's hardly a King's ransom is it, Dad.'

'Lucy, how much are those packets of Doggie Treats?'

'Ninety-nine pence each, why?'

'So he's got four more packets then he had twenty minutes ago hasn't he? When we collect the winnings, yes!'

It was getting dark again and the Ritsons bade their farewells. They hadn't left their own lights on and the three little Yorkies would need a walkies and a wee soon anyway. Shirley glanced back at the front of the Wendover with its illuminated neon sign. She just couldn't imagine it saying Hotel Scarbados! Then suddenly, out of the blue, she had a flashback.

'I say, Garry, I've just thought. Do you remember that short-lived TV series called 'Scarborough'?

'Vaguely, yes on BBC I think. That's right. Brilliant photography using drones. Not much of a plot though if I recall and it was abandoned after six episodes.'

'Yes, that's the one, why?'

'Well, I've just remembered what happened a few days after the last episode was shown.'

'Yeah what?'

'Well I was listening to BBC Radio York, as I always do when I'm busy in the kitchen, and a chap called in from Scarborough to talk about it with the presenter, Jonathan somebody, it's a while ago now. Anyway he said that in his opinion they should change the scriptwriters, change the programme's name to SCARBADOS and give it another go. It didn't happen though did it?'

'Obviously not but you know maybe young Millie's idea wasn't so outlandish as you first thought.'

'We'll have to wait and see won't we? One thing's for sure, they're keen to get weaving. When all the Covid restrictions are over there'll be no stopping them. I'm sure of that. Watch this space eh?'

20.

Christmas, such as it was for the Fishburns, was over. They had made the very best of difficult circumstances and thanks to lovely neighbours had celebrated in their new surroundings. With the unpacking complete and the contents roughly where they were going to eventually end up, it was time to look forward to the task ahead. Covid rules, regulations and restrictions were still enforced but they could at least plan and put some things into place ready for when they could start trading as a bona-fide business. They would be the new kids on the block but perhaps starting with a blank canvas, not to mention new ideas, would give them a few yards start over their immediate competitors. Once again Millie took the helm and straight after breakfast on New Year's Eve she ushered her father into the conservatory with that arc-lever file labelled Hotel Scarbados Business Plan. They were on their own. Just the two of them, a small table, two dining room chairs – and all those Palms and Yucca trees. It was a grey morning and they had the ceiling lights on at their end of the large conservatory. Both radiators were switched on full blast.

'I'm glad you put the heating on, love. It's a tad colder than Hull I think where we are here. Never mind the gas bill eh?'

'Actually Dad, I want us to have the heating on for the next twenty-eight days.'

'You want to what?'

'Yes and full blast. This is the coldest time of the year and the forecast is for the chill to continue for the foreseeable future. I want to see how much our energy costs will be as a worst possible scenario. I've sent in meter readings online. Whether we continue with the current providers remains to be seen. On the thirty-first of January I'll read them again and we'll get several quotes OK?'

'Millie, you're the only member of this family who can tackle this. You do know that don't you?'

'I'm coming to that, Dad. It's important that we decide our respective roles. It's a classic family business, on paper anyway. If rumours in the MSM are correct then ...'

'The what? M S what?'

'Main stream media. You'll have to get used to all this jargon Dad.'

'Anyway, according to rumours all Covid related restrictions are going to be lifted just immediately before Easter, which is early this year. Easter Sunday is the last day of March and you know what that means don't you?'

'Do enlighten me!'

'Lighter nights! It's the day after the clocks go forward. Folks start to come out of hibernation after the long winter and take their first real break of the new year. We must prepare for that. Add to that the fact that folks will be able to travel about again will make it even an bigger 'rush to the coast' than normal.'

'Like a Klondike Gold Rush except its sand instead of gold.'

'Exactly, Scarborough will be absolutely heaving I guarantee it. Even if it pees down from Good Friday to Easter Monday. It won't just be Scarborough either. It's going to be the same all over the country from Brid to Bournemouth and Torquay to Tynemouth. Trust me. But anyway, back to what I was about to say. What are going to be our respective duties? Don't forget this is now a business. We've all got to pull our weight based on our skills and strengths.' Pete suddenly looked gloomy.

'Millie, I'm sorry but I don't think I have any real strengths. What can I offer?' Millie almost exploded, uncharacteristically for her.

'Dad, you're wrong, wrong wrong. You have lots to offer but maybe it takes someone else to point it out to you. For twenty years, in fact since just before I came into this world, what did you do at work? I'll remind you shall I? You dealt with hundreds of people every day on that ferry. How many hundreds of thousands is that over two decades. And even if you only dealt with a hundred a day I make that over a half a million during the time you served. So the bottom line is that you know how to deal with people of every social background. I'll bet many of them you served many times too. Yes?'

'You're right there. Lots of folks made that crossing every month – even if it was just to buy booze and tobacco. Many of them became personal friends over the years, mainly Hull folks but lots from York, Brid and even around here. Is it relevant?'

'Of course it is, Dad. It's called repeat business! That's what a good hotel is all about. Loyal customers.'

'Anyway, you will make an excellent front of house. Running the small Bar will be an absolute doddle for you. Won't it?'

'I guess so and serving a maximum of thirty-two guests, assuming a hundred percent occupancy in the summer months should be easy.'

'Dad, you've made two incorrect assumptions already and we've hardly started on the Plan have we?'

'Really? What assumptions?'

'Firstly that the Bar is only going to be open to residents and secondly that the hotel will only be full in the summer months. I'm looking for eighty percent occupancy all the year round not just July and August.'

'You've been busy behind the scenes haven't you? What about the Licence itself. Did the Wendover have a Licence, if so what sort.'

'I've already made provisional enquiries with the Licensing Officer at the Town Hall. She's called Melanie and was very helpful.'

'What? When did you do that?'

'Yesterday. They're all working from home of course via laptops and PCs but yesterday was still an official work day. She told me that it isn't as simple as picking Licence A or Licence B either. She looked into their records and then told me that the Wendover did have a Residents Licence but that it was rescinded after irregularities came to light and get this, there was a major incident that happened here that brought about the cancellation not just of the Licence but that the Hotel was closed for almost a week pending police investigations.'

'Good Lord, well that wasn't in the Sales Prospectus was it? So what exactly happened did she say any more?'

'She was reluctant to talk about it over the phone. She's been in the job for years and never seen or heard anything like it.'

'What no other information at all?'

'Oh yes, she's originally from Newcastle, has two grown-up kids who now live down south, has a black Labrador called Jet and …'

'Good grief. How long were you on the phone for?'

'Oh about twenty minutes. She was obviously bored stiff

working from home. She says she'll pop round with the necessary paperwork the next time she brings Jet for a walk around Peasholm Park. She says she'll tell me more then over a coffee. And all this reminds me – you will of course be the official Licence Holder and thus the de facto landlord.

Now, let's move on shall we, Dad? Mum and Lucy will be in charge of Housekeeping which brings me to Jamie. What do you see as his role in the future Hotel Scarbados? What is he good at? Is he going to enrol in further education or what when everything's back to normal? Has he even talked about it with you and Mum?' Pete started to look a little melancholy.

'Millie, looking back, I don't think I've been a particularly good Dad to Jamie. Being at sea for so many days a year isn't conducive to being a good parent. Apart from taking him to watch "The Tigers" whenever we were in port on Saturday afternoon, I think I've failed miserably. My only son too. He's a nice lad and a good lad and in a few months he'll be a legal adult. Sorry to admit this but you know him better than I do. Got any ideas?'

'Actually, Dad, as it happens I do.'

'Go on then, Millie, do tell me. I'm all ears.'

'Dad, with respect, I think it's best I have a quiet word with him on my own. You know, Big Sis and all that. If that's OK with you?'

That's what Pete liked about all his kids. They all looked out for each other and he was truly grateful for that, he really was. He was closer to Millie, his first-born, but he always knew that when he was away, which was most of the time, the family was always a bond.

'OK, I'll leave that bit with you. Now, what else is on your Agenda? What about Sales & Advertising ready for when we can actually open as a business. I've seen some old copies of the Scarborough Guide and it seems that nearly every hotel and B & B in the area advertises in it. I'm sure we could soon knock a photograph and a few words together.' Millie sighed.

'No, Dad, no. Covid has changed all that forever. What if Covid comes back again in another form or even a new epidemic altogether? Paying good money for advance advertising might prove to be a total waste of money. No, we'll advertise online only – at least for the first year.'

'You mean advertise on other peoples' websites such as …'

'No, Dad, on our own website.'

'What? We'd better get a wiggle on then before somebody else copies our idea. Get your laptop out and Google www.hotelscarbados.com. Go on, do it.'

Millie smiled and just for once, without argument, did as she was asked.

'Look see. I told you! That domain's reserved! We should have done it already.'

'Dad, I did it before we'd even moved, in fact before we'd even exchanged contracts. It's registered in my name. If those rumours are right then we've got ninety days to turn this from an idea to reality. That's not long. Yes, we'll need new photos for the website you bet. I know somebody on the same course as me who builds neat websites and she'll have a ball with Hotel Scarbados, trust me. But of course whilst we can take digital pictures of the interior we can't do the exterior until the new neon sign is designed, fixed and working. Now can we? Can I leave that one with you, Dad? Please.'

'Sure, once you've taught me how to use this laptop. You know how long it took for you to teach me how to use an iPhone.' Millie giggled.

'You can say that again. But you're slowly getting the hang of technology. Start looking now – just Google *'illuminated neon signs'* and follow your nose. Let's you and I sit down again a week from today and review progress. Yes? And by then it'll be eighty-nine days to go, just remember that.'

Pete just smiled and wondered what Millie had in mind for his only son. He'd love to be a fly on the wall but there again perhaps not. Young adults need privacy too.

21.

It was just after dusk and Jamie came back from a long walk with Seb.

'Hiya, Sis. Wow that was our longest walk yet. Seb's knackered and I'm not far behind. What's for tea and who's cooking today?'

'Well it was your turn according to the rota. Where've you been? It's dark. Did you get lost?'

'No, went down to the sea front and turned left past those swanky looking apartments -hardly anybody about. Just the odd person with a dog. Then we walked along past all those beach chalets, you know all those multi-coloured ones you see on pictures and postcards. We should have turned round and come back the same way but we didn't.'

'So where the heck did you end up?'

'We turned left and ended up going right through the grounds of the Open Air Theatre. Amazing! All closed for the winter of course, not to mention Covid, but some of the old posters were still up. All weather-beaten of course but you could still read most of them.'

Like what?'

'The stars that had performed there before lock-down.'

'Let me guess. Showaddywaddy, Dana, Acker Bilk, Dusty Springfield ...'

'No, stop taking the Michael you. I'm talking Kylie Minogue, Elton John, Britney Spears ... the list goes on and on.'

'Gosh, I'd no idea. And it's just ten minutes walk away right?'

'Yes, in fact not even that. We haven't really got our bearings yet have we? Thanks to Covid restrictions.'

'I know but we'll get there, Jamie, we'll get there. Listen, pop the kettle on bro and bring two nice mugs of tea into the conservatory. Need a little chat – just between us two OK?'

'Sure. I'll clean up Seb's paws too. At least he hasn't been digging round that flippin' tree again. Not for a few days anyway. Give me five.'

'Jamie, I was chatting to Dad earlier and he seemed to have lost a bit of confidence and how he was going to slot into the scheme of things. And then I got to thinking about you. How do you see your role?' Jamie took a long slurp of his tea.

'I'm not sure Sis. In fact I'm not sure that I'm going to slot in at all. Dad will have to show me how to do the Bar work when he's not here or having a day off. I can't think much beyond that to be honest. It all seems so far away.'

'OK I want to put an idea to you but it's only an idea. Your A-levels have been completely cocked up by Covid, not to mention our move from Hull to Scarborough …'

'Siss, I'm not going back to Sixth Form in Hull when it's all over. I'm just not OK? Mum and Dad will be livid I know. My predicted grades were already below par and now it'll be even worse.'

'Jamie, apart from Match of the Day, what's your favourite TV programme?'

'You know the answer to that already – Master Chef!'

'Exactly! So if I told you that Scarborough TEC has a terrific reputation for its Catering Diploma and that its courses will re-commence as soon as Covid is over would you be interested in finding out a bit more?'

'Wow! What? I didn't know that. Are you sure?'

'Oh yes. Take a look at their website. You can make initial enquiries online. Just promise me you'll think about it.'

'You bet I will, but its strictly between us two all-right Not a word to anyone else in the family. Not for now anyway. Promise?'

'I promise Bro. Now, any more tea in the pot? Lucy's making tea by the way. It's scrambled eggs on toast with grilled bacon.'

'Crikey is that it? With a bit more imagination it could be Eggs Royale, Eggs Benedict or even …'

Millie smiled. It sounded like he had taken the bait already. She didn't tell him that she had already spoken on the phone to the Department Head at the TEC. He didn't need to know, at least not yet anyway. Jamie had always been a bit 'backward in coming forward' and from time to time he needed a little push. That time was now. As soon as they were allowed to open the Hotel Scarbados it would be on a B & B basis for the time being but it would only be a matter of time before they would have to offer food in the evening too. This was her real plan for Jamie but she kept that bit to herself for now. One step at a time.

22.

'Hi, Melanie, it's so nice to meet you. Please come in. We're not quite straight yet but we're getting there – I think.'

"Melanie from Licensing" as she was known at the Town Hall, had kept her promise to bring the relevant forms to the Wendover on Saturday morning.

'Here's those forms to fill in I promised you. They're quite straightforward but give me a call on my mobile if you get stuck OK? I've scribbled it on a post-it note. The main decision you have to make is whether you get a residents only Licence or one that allows you to serve alcohol to non-residents as well.'

'Melanie, please come in for a coffee and we can have a quick chat ..'

'I'd love to but I've got Jet in the car and I can hear him barking already. With all this working from home malarkey he's been used to being in my company for months now. So Covid has affected animals as well as humans hasn't it?'

'I think you're right but our dog, Seb, has always had one or more of us around him. Hey, I've just had an idea. Where are you taking Jet for a walk? Into Peasholm Park did you say?'

'Well that was my original idea but I've changed my mind. We're going to Scalby Mills. The tide's out and Jet just loves a "walkies" along the sand. Does Seb like sand? Some dogs don't apparently. Look, how about you follow me and bring Seb with you in your car. We can't travel together because we're not in the same bubble. Bonkers if you ask me but hey-ho.'

'Fab idea. I'll go and get Seb and the car keys and tell Dad I'll be about an hour do you think?'

'Great. I'll wait until you reverse out before I start off. It's not far. The car park's free until around Easter time so don't worry.'

Five minutes later and they set off northwards in a convoy of two. They arrived at the Council owned car park within ten minutes and parked in parallel facing the sea.

'Wow, what a view, Mel. Can I call you Mel?'

'Most people do so, sure, that's fine by me. Do you know where you are? You can't have been here long.'

'Less than a month. It's just flown by. Goodness me, what on Earth is that big white building over there? They look like pyramids.'

'You mean you don't know? It's on TV quite a lot – hadn't you noticed? It's the famous Scarborough Sea Life Centre.'

'No, to be honest. We've moved from Hull where the regional TV was linked more to Humberside and North Lincolnshire. We're tuned into BBC Yorkshire now that Dad finally managed the tuning process on the remote control!'

'So did you see a couple of days ago the Centre was on the news on national TV, not just Yorkshire.'

'No, we've been so busy getting the hotel ship-shape as Dad puts it. He used to work on the ferries from Hull until he got made redundant. That's the main reason we moved here. Why was it on the news?'

'It was really interesting and heart-warming. A small loggerhead turtle had been washed up on the Scottish Island of Iona. It was half-dead but some marine biologists rescued it and cared for it for months. Then it was brought here to Scarborough right here a hundred yards from where we're standing now. After a year it was brought back to full health and a couple of days ago was released into warmer waters in Portugal where it should have landed following it's trans-Atlantic crossing.'

'Oh wow, what a lovely story.'

'Ah yes, but it's not a story. It's real. They do wonderful work here with rescued seals as well.'

'Just wait until I tell me little sister Lucy about this place. She's animal mad. Anyway what was that you were going to tell me about the Wendover and the problems with the Licence?'

'Well, this is strictly off the record of course but as a lot of it was leaked to the papers and social media I guess I can tell the gist of it all. The Wendover got quite a reputation for special events and other types of gatherings.'

'You mean like birthday parties and stuff?'

'Well yes but things like Murder Mystery Nights and Fawlty Towers weekends. They held them quite often, maybe once a month. It was good for business that's for sure. Extra Bar-takings would have proved useful particularly in the winter months between New Year and Easter – in fact where we are now except nobody had even heard of Covid.'

'Sounds good from a financial point of view.'

'No doubt but the breach of regulations cropped up when somebody made an anonymous complaint about late night noise and the number of late-night drinkers. An undercover colleague, in fact someone from County Hall, posed as a guest and counted over eighty drinkers. Even at full occupancy there would only have been thirty-two at a maximum. The owners pleaded ignorance but they must have thought we were born yesterday. A fine was levied and a new upgraded Licence was issued.'

'Was that a criminal offence? How come the Police were involved?'

'Oh no, that was much later. According to social media a Murder Mystery Night went wrong. The hotel proprietors could select from half a dozen murder scripts written by the organisers. A lady called Coletta from memory, but that might not have been her real name. Anyway the 'Whodunit' finished about ten in the evening and a late night supper was served to all those attending.'

'So what's illegal about that? They had the right Licence by then didn't they?'

'Yes, but wait for this, at breakfast the next morning one of the guests was missing – a chap in his late seventies from Lancashire. It was a locally employed part-time breakfast waitress who took his 'Tea, toast and Telegraph' to his single table and he wasn't there. A search of his room and the whole hotel proved fruitless. The Police were called and every guest was interviewed. The Press, you know what they're like, tried to suggest the title of the evening 'Murder in the Lake' might have tipped the old boy over the edge. Lancashire Police became involved and his wife was also interviewed in Bolton. Seems like they were estranged and had long-term financial problems. The bar-tender confirmed that he'd been drinking heavily that night.'

'Gosh, so what happened then?'

'There was a right carry-on. Police divers searched the lake in Peasholm Park. Nothing. HM Coast Guards helicopters searched the immediate coast-line in case he'd done a "Reginald Perrin" and tried to walk to Denmark. Still nothing. The Coroner Recorded an open verdict. The Wendover never really recovered its reputation after that.

It traded for a few more months then closed suddenly. The owners left to go abroad I believe. If it was me I'd change the name of the Hotel and give it a fresh start. Give it some thought before you complete the Application, Millie. I would.'

'Actually, we don't have to. It's new name is Hotel Scarbados!'

'Wow! That's brill! Come on, let's take Seb and Jet down onto the beach. We've done enough yacking I reckon don't you?'

Unlike Jet, who splashed around on the edge of the water, Seb didn't take to it at all. In fact he didn't seem to like sand, wet or dry. He just wanted to get back home to his tree and have a pee on home territory as it were.

They walked back to their cars, leads were undone, and canines placed on board.

'Thanks for all your help, Mel. We'll fill those forms in soon as soon as the change of name is official. And as for the goss, well what can I say?'

'You're welcome. Good luck and welcome to Scarbados!'

'If all goes to plan, would you like to come to our Opening Night?'

'Oh I'd love to. Just make sure you've got the correct Licence in place. You know what bureaucrats can be like. Ha ha!'

Ten minutes later and Millie was back home at the soon to be renamed Wendover. Seb went straight to 'his tree' for a wee and managed to dig another three inches towards Alice Springs before Lucy called him in. He always listened to her. She gave him more treats than the others.

'Mum, Dad, you won't believe what I've got to tell you!'

Millie told them everything that "Mel from Licensing" had told her.

23.

'Well, I guess that explains why the hotel's income started to tail off. Maybe it wasn't illness at all that forced the sale, Millie.' Pete and Mandy were open-minded, particularly Pete.

'At the end of the day does it matter? Not really. We bought the Wendover at a good price and whether that was because of illness, a falling market or Covid, it matters not.' To the others' surprise Mandy suddenly turned.

'I told you we shouldn't have moved on a Friday – it's bad luck. In fact the more I think about it the more I think we should have stayed in Hull and …'

'Hey, Mum, come on. It'll get better. Covid won't last forever and as soon as we're allowed to open properly we'll take off like a rocket. Won't we Dad?' The steely look in Millie's eyes pleaded for a positive response to placate and reassure her Mother. It was the first time she had visibly mouthed any negative thoughts on the project.

'By the way, Mum, you mentioned you'd come across some receipts and invoices in a drawer. Let's hope it's the former – we don't need any more bills to pay. Not yet anyway.'

'Oh no, but wait a sec and I'll get them. Look, here's the invoice from the firm that installed the illuminated Wendover Hotel sign three years ago. They're called We are Neon Ltd. and they're in Middlesbrough. How far away is that?'

Pete's geography was better than anyone else's and he'd previously served as skeleton crew when his ferry had gone into dry-dock in Teesport for a routine paint job and anti-fouling.

'It's about fifty miles. Just over an hour's drive maybe. There's a number and I'll call it now. They could still be closed of course, with staff on furlough. I'll try it now, you never know.' Not unexpectedly it was an answer-phone.

'This is We are Neon. Thank you for calling. Our office is only manned part-time during lock-down but we are still managing to provide a limited service depending on the size of the job and social distancing. Please leave a name and number and we'll get back to you.'

Pete left a short but succinct message and his mobile number. They still hadn't arranged a land-line and it was on the 'to do' list along with other matters such as a computer and a copier for the reception area.

'We might get these guys to look at new lighting for the dining room and the conservatory if they do that sort of stuff. The conservatory needs to look and feel more like Kew Gardens, or even Barbados, by the time we open.'

To everyone's surprise Pete's mobile rang just a few seconds after he had replaced it in his pocket.

'Hello, Peter Fishburn.'

'Hi, it's Dave Gibson here, returning your call from We are Neon. Sorry I couldn't reach my phone when I heard it ringing. It was under a mountain of paperwork on my desk. I'm not the the best when it comes to paperwork. Our office girl says she's working from home but how she can do that when all the quotes are here is beyond me. Anyway, that's my problem. How can I help you Mr Fishburn?'

'Thank you for getting back to me so quickly. We've recently taken over ownership of a small hotel here in Scarborough and we want to change the name of the hotel from the Wendover to the Hotel …'

'Wow. The Wendover did you say? Near Peasholm Park?'

'Yes. From the date of the invoice your firm fixed the exterior neon light just over three years ago. It doesn't say 'Paid' on the invoice though from what I can see.'

'No, it won't do. They didn't pay it. Very odd people if you ask me. You know, dodgy, more than a bit shifty.'

'I'm sorry to hear that Mr Gibson. If you'd rather we looked elsewhere in the circumstances I would quite understand.'

'No, it's not your fault. We'd be happy to quote once we know the specs. Have you got an order number there?'

'Yes, here it is.'

'Give me a minute while I check on the computer file. I'll keep talking while I punch some keys on the key-board. Yep – here it is WendoverHotel. There was only just room for thirteen characters so no space for a gap, you know like those racehorse names that are words all joined together. They're only allowed seventeen characters including any gaps, did you know that?'

'Can't say I did but you learn something every day.'

'What's the new name of your hotel please?'

'Hotel Scarbados.'

'Heck. I love the name but that's even longer. Can I suggest that you split it with the word hotel in small letters above with Scarbados in bigger capital letters below? It will add to the cost of course but it would look great. And can I suggest that you change the colour to anything but red?'

'Why?'

'Well when we came to do the job it was all a bit fishy. There were at least a half a dozen attractive Eastern European girls staying there even though it was winter. Lots of Poles and Rumanian girls work in the hospitality industry of course but in a small hotel I would have thought there was no need. It's not that big a place is it? Anyway on the drive back up after the job was done my young apprentice jokingly said – 'well now we know why they wanted a red light don't we?' But looking back many a true word is spoken in jest. He might have been right.'

'Oh my God. It get's worse. Only today we heard that an elderly resident went missing, never to be seen again. You're right, let's make it a dark green sign instead and give it a completely new look.'

'Leave it with me and I'll get back to you with a quote in a day or two.'

'Great. Thanks for your help.'

Pete hung up. He'd forgotten that his mobile was in 'speaker' mode. Mandy was in tears.

'What else can go wrong? Now it looks like we've unwittingly bought a house of ill-repute. Just who were these people for God's sake? We should have looked into the background of this whole place and the owners before we bought it with my money?' She spat out the last two words with vitriol. Mandy and Pete were both equally taken aback. Did she really mean that or was the general all-round situation just getting to her. Millie reacted first.

'Aw come on, Mam. We'll soon have the new sign, a new name, a new image and new clients. Let's put the kettle on.'

'Lucy's taken Seb out for a walk but where on Earth has your brother gone? I heard him starting up his motor-bike. There's still work to do here, doesn't he know that? Never mind sight-seeing.'

'Don't be too hard on him, Mam. We're all still trying to adjust in our own way aren't we?'

Millie knew exactly where he was but for the moment that was a little secret between the two of them. As they spoke Jamie was indeed on his bike and heading south from the Town Centre on the Filey Road. He'd checked on Google maps before he set out. Two miles later and he turned right into the small campus that used to be called the Teacher's Training College, now Scarborough TEC. There were only a handful of cars parked in the large car park and he left his bike in a slot marked 'staff only' as there wouldn't be many staff working that's for sure. He dismounted and took off his helmet. Within seconds a middle-aged chap emerged from a side-door.'

'Can I help you, young man? The College is still officially closed you know.'

'Yes but tomorrow I've got an unofficial interview with the Head of Catering. I'm new to the area and I thought I'd do a little recce first to make sure I'm at the right place and not late on the day.'

'That's what I call planning lad. I'll show you. Just come round to this smart-looking door. It's locked at the moment but if you peek through the glass you can see what's inside. Look.'

'Crickey, it looks like a posh restaurant!'

'It doesn't just look like one lad, it is one. It's called 'Nineteen09' after the year it was constructed. It's where the catering students learn their trade and how to become first class chefs or restaurateurs. Best in't country so I'm led to believe. Anyway I'd best be off. Good look tomorrow.'

Jamie was on his bike but had he been on foot he would have had a spring in his step all the way back home. He couldn't wait to tell Big Sis what he'd just seen.

24.

The nameplate on the modest office said Samantha Lyon, Head of Department. Jamie knocked twice, fairly softly. It was ten o'clock and he was bang on time thanks to yesterday's reconnaissance trip. Punctuality was something his father had always instilled in him – sailing times, twenty-four hour clocks and all that.

'Come in, you must be Jamie Fishburn. I'd shake hands but we're not in the same bubble are we?'

They both laughed and instantly the ice was broken. Any nerves Jamie might have had melted like late spring snowflakes.

'Please. Take a seat. I'll organise us some tea in a minute. Milk and sugar?' Jamie wasn't expecting this.

'And can I take your jacket. It looks like a biker's jacket to me. Am I right?'

She already knew it was just that as she'd spotted him the day before from her office window. She already had the impression Jamie must be a 'bit of a planner.' Most young folks today wouldn't have bothered and just left it chance that they would find the place and not worry too much if they were a bit late. The tea arrived.

'Now, Jamie, what sort of tea do you think this is?'

'You mean like Sainsburys or Yorkshire tea? It tastes like the tea we use at home. Yorkshire tea. Why?'

'You're right but here we try to encourage our students to distinguish between various types such as Morning

Breakfast tea, Afternoon tea etc. and that's before we get on to speciality teas such as Earl Grey and the like. You look a bit puzzled.'

'Well I thought this where you can learn to cook not learn about fancy teas.'

'Jamie, you saw that restaurant downstairs didn't you? We don't teach you how to fry bacon and eggs. We can teach you how to run a first class eatery. Now, tell me about your new family hotel. What's it called again? The Barbados or something?' She was deliberately playing with him.

'It's called the Hotel Scarbados actually, just a play on words. My sister Millie's idea. What do you think to it?'

'Well it sounds a bit chavish to me to be honest but if you're hoping to add a slightly Caribbean theme to it then how are you going to incorporate that theme in your menus? If at all?'

'I'm not sure it hasn't been discussed much yet and we might only do B & B for the first few months.'

'In my opinion that would be a huge mistake. You have to set yourselves apart from the rest of the hundreds of small B & B's that cater for what I call the lower orders of this country. If all you're going to offer is bacon & eggs, white or brown toast with a pot of Yorkshire tea then the Hotel Scarbados will just be in with the 'also rans'. Here's a pen and paper. Whilst I'm going to get some more tea. I want you to write down your idea of a quality breakfast menu. See you shortly.'

By the time she returned Jamie's list read as follows:

Your choice of Speciality Teas or Coffee
Cereals and Fruit Juices
Full English Breakfasts
Toast or Bread Rolls.

'Mmm, well I suppose it's a start, Jamie. But look at this one here which is our standard breakfast menu that we practice with students downstairs at Nineteen09.' She reached into a drawer and handed him a laminated menu. It was somewhat up-market from Jamie's efforts.

Breakfast teas and Speciality teas upon request.
Freshly ground Free Trade coffee – Javan or Kenyan
Locally smoked Kippers or Kedgeree
Free range eggs from our own local source
cooked to your order
Yorkshire bacon and Rare Breed pork sausages
Eggs Benedict or Eggs Royale
A selection of breads and rolls (including Gluten free)
Croissants
Toast or French toast
Yorkshire butter or a selection of Vegan spreads
Jams, marmalades and preserves – low sugar upon request.

Bon Appetit.

'Oh heck. What is kedgeree? Never even heard of it!'

'It was very popular in Victorian times and its a mixture of rice, fish and eggs and looks a bit like a risotto. Not awfully keen myself but the fact that it's even on the menu gives you Brownie points. Hardly anyone ever asks for it.'

'I'm not surprised.'

'So, Jamie, if this was your menu on the day the Hotel Scarbados opens how would you fare? Have a think and be honest with me.' Jamie scanned down the list and pondered.

'Well I could cope with most of it. No chance with the Kedgeree and some coaching with the two egg dishes. But apart from that …'

'OK Jamie, I'll come clean with you. The Covid epidemic has played hell with our academic routine. With lock-down, half of our students have already deserted their courses and won't return. Even if restrictions are lifted at Easter, which we all hope for, one full term just isn't enough to complete the syllabus. So, I am going to suggest to my bosses that, as an experiment, we inaugurate a short three month crash-course in basic catering and food hygiene. Add to the Covid situation that dozens of European staff left the UK for good after Brexit and it all added up to a nightmare for hotels, schools and even Care Homes. Only yesterday I had a Nursing Home Manager on the phone almost pleading with me to provide experienced cooks. It's awful. I'll come straight to the point, Jamie. If I get a green light from the bosses I want to start the first of these short courses as soon as all restrictions are lifted. Are you interested? Yes or no?' His reply was unexpected.

'Has the Pope got a balcony?'

She pondered later that they must have a different sense of humour in Hull.

'Can I take this menu home with me please? It'll give me something to think about and work on.'

'Of course you can, Jamie. And I want you to start thinking about seven signature dishes that you might like to see on the Hotel evening menus.'

'Really? OK I'll give it some thought. What do I do now?'

'Go home. Think about what we've just discussed. Make plans. Talk to your family. As soon as the Covid restrictions are lifted the fastest runners out of the blocks stand to gain the most. Don't forget, millions of people have been virtually locked up against their will for months. The coast is where they'll head for first. Assuming another Beast from the East doesn't arrive.'

'A what from the East?'

'A Beast. A once in a lifetime perfect storm that hit the Yorkshire Coast a few years back.'

'Never heard of it. Anyway thanks for everything.'

As soon as she heard the motorbike roar out of the College car park Samantha picked up the phone.

'Hi Millie, just to tell you that your brother Jamie has just left. How did it go? Brilliantly I would say but he'll probably be a few days before it all fully sinks in.'

'Thanks Sam, we owe you one. Hey, how about coming to our Opening Evening – when it finally arrives that is?'

'Thank you, I'd love to. Hey, I'm thinking out loud here but how about the College becoming involved in some way? I could get some of our students to help lay on a buffet. It would be a great experience for them, I know it would. Oh, by the way, did the Pope ever visit Hull?'

'No idea, why?'

'Never mind, I'll tell you some time. 'Bye and thanks again.'

'Cheers.'

25.

Jamie had barely got home and put his bike away before Millie came running out the back door to greet him.

'How did it go, Bro.' she said as if it was a chorus line in a song. She played dumb and didn't let on about her conversations, two now, with the helpful Samantha Lyon.'

'Yeah OK I guess. Quite good in fact.'

'So are you gonna tell me or leave me in mid-air?'

'Sis, let's take a little stroll around the garden shall we and have a chat. The weather's fine at least. Look there, look! Some crocuses are poking through. The first sign that winter's coming to an end and spring isn't far away.'

'Well that's what Granny Johnson used to say isn't it. Mum misses her terribly you know. You can see it in her eyes when she talks about her.'

'Yes, it shows. In fact any mention of Hull at all seems to dampen her eyes. At times I do often wonder whether the move to Scarborough was a good thing for her. Great for us in the long term but I do worry about Mum.'

'She misses her sisters and spends hours on the phone to them chatting about the old days in Hull – you know, where they shopped and went for coffees on a Saturday. By comparison Scarborough's a small place.'

'Yes but when the trains are back to normal it's only just over an hour away. She can go there every other Saturday or they can come here, surely?'

'Yes, or even meet in Beverley. They all love Beverley.'

'Don't we all? It's like a mini-York isn't it? You know with a Minster and lots of history.'

'Anyway we'll all have to keep an eye on her, that's for sure. Mental health has become a major issue during lockdown and we don't want to see our own Mam suffer under our own eyes.'

Their conversation was interrupted by their father's voice bellowing out from the back door.

'Come you two. We've just got some news. Dave from We are Neon has just been on the blower. Since we accepted his quote for the new Hotel Scarbados sign he's been working flat out. If it's convenient for us he's coming to remove the old one and put up the new one tomorrow morning. All we have to do is observe social distancing between us and his colleague. I told him that's fine by us. What do you think?'

For Millie this was a huge step in the right direction – another piece in the huge jigsaw that was project Hotel Scarbados. With the new sign, the website could be completed and put online once the photographs had been taken. She must remember to speak with him about new lighting for the conservatory now that the palms and yuccas seem to have acclimatised to their new home. They had decided not to plant them outdoors as it seems that they had been bred, like hybrids, to be indoor trees. She had seen some examples of We are Neon's work on their website and was very impressed.

'That's great news, Dad. What did Mam say?'

'Not a lot to be honest. I think she was on her own mobile yacking to one of her sisters. What on Earth do they find to yack about?' If only they knew.

Tea that day was a 'spag bol' made with quorn to placate Lucy. It gave Jamie more to think about than his 'seven signature dishes' that Samantha Lyon had told him to concentrate on. Why seven he wondered? Why not six, or eight or even ten. He wasn't quite on the same wavelength yet as his future tutor but he would be pretty soon. He just didn't know it yet. After cups of tea and cheese and biscuits they chilled out in front of the TV. There was still a glimmer of light outside and Mandy came out with the same line that she always did at this time of year.

'My Mam used to say that by the second Sunday in February you can eat your tea at five o'clock without putting a light on.'

'Well hopefully this time tomorrow we'll be able to test out the new light won't we? Said Millie. 'I'll get my camera ready to send some shots to my mate Katya who's building the website for us. Then as soon as the new lighting in the conservatory is finished we can add that onto the website too. It's going to look like Barbados in there even if we are at fifty three degrees north and not …'

'Thirteen north' chipped in Peter, ever the geographer. And by the way how much extra is that going to cost? You never mentioned this in the Business Plan, Millie.'

She decided not to reply. There was a bit of leeway built into the costings and they both knew it. Another grand wouldn't hurt as long as they got off to a good start with business takings. All they needed now was an end to Covid restrictions and the loss of personal freedom. They weren't alone. It was something the whole country was praying for. Hancock's Half Hour was becoming a daily drudge but millions watched it simply because they had nothing better to do.

Jamie stayed up late playing with his iPad looking at snippets of Master Chef on YouTube. Secretly he was totally enthused. He fell asleep and dreamt of white aprons and chefs' hats.

Breakfast the next morning was a bit more exciting than the normal cornflakes, tea and toast. Eggs Benedict appeared on the table for all five of them, minus the ham or bacon for Lucy of course.

'Jamie, can't we get vegetarian bacon? You know my preferences these days.'

'I don't know, Lucy. We'll have to see what's available once we get into the swing of things with the 'cash and carry' won't we. And can you explain why you veggies and vegans want artificial meat to look like real meat?'

She didn't answer but just scowled at him like sisters do to older brothers.

'What do you think, Mam. Does it meet with your approval?'

'I don't know where you get these fancy ideas from, I really don't. When my own Mam did a bit of B & B or took in lodgers to make ends meet it was cornflakes and eggs on toast. Porridge in the winter. Folks today don't know they're born. And when did you say that chap was coming from Middlesbrough with that fancy new sign? A waste of time and money if you ask me.'

Nobody said anything. The silence was deafening.

The We are Neon Transit van arrived mid-morning and Dave Gibson and his colleague, a young lad around twenty, opened up the rear doors after reversing into the drive. It was a relatively mild morning with a milky sun poking through the leafless trees on the other side of the road. For the first time that Spring their own palms outside the front door actually did look like they belonged to another world. The world of 'Scarbados' perhaps. Dave was in jovial mood.

'Morning all. A nice day for it. Any chance of a couple of coffees? We were in such a rush we left our Thermos flasks in the workshop.' Millie obliged. After all this was her baby and she just couldn't wait to see the new sign in action. It's affixing would be the first real manifestation that ideas were at last becoming a reality. Dave and his young apprentice sprung into action without delay.

'Right let's get these ladders off the van roof. Thank goodness we don't need scaffolding. Another metre or so and the Health and Safety brigade would have delayed us for weeks. Pete, make sure the power's turned off now please. We'll be taking the old Wendover sign down within a few minutes and of course we'll have to disconnect its power supply first. Hopefully we'll be able to use the same electrical connectors as we did for the old sign. That's the plan anyway. I seem to remember it was very heavy and it took two of us to put it up using two separate ladders. It's all coming back now. We'll unscrew the two retaining bolts one at a time OK. We don't want to do a Dell-Boy like they did when that chandelier came crashing down now do we?'

Thirty minutes later and the old sign was safely lowered to the ground in one piece.

'Where shall we put it? It's not the easiest thing to take to the tip, even if it was open.'

'In the shed out the back please, for now anyway. It's not the sort of thing you can use again is it?'

An hour later and the new Hotel Scarbados sign was in place. It looked absolutely fabulous even before being switched on .

'OK put the power back on please. The five small letters of 'hotel' flickered first for a second or two followed by the much larger nine capital letters of SCARBADOS. Even in the dappled sunshine it stood out. They all came outside to see it for the first time. All that is except Mandy. She was in the conservatory reading a magazine.

'Right, Pete, we'll be off to the next job then. Two more to do in Brid. When the lock-down is declared over the whole of the coast is gonna go bananas!' Millie stopped him.

'We've got another job for you to look at and quote for please, Mr Gibson.'

'I don't know! Just when I wanted a bit of peace and quiet as well. You lot come barging in. What new-fangled scheme have you come up with now for goodness sake? I'm going into the lounge!'

'Sorry about that Mr Gibson. Mam's a bit frayed at the moment.'

'Well aren't we all to be fair. The last year or more has been weird. Time means nothing. We only just survived as a business thanks to that furlough arrangement. It's good job I had paid myself a modest salary from the firm and not relied on dividends as the main shareholder. I'd have had to shut the business for good and with a wife and two nippers I'd have been at the food banks like thousands of others. What a state the country's in. Now what exactly did you have in mind? Can you switch on the existing lights fully please?'

'They're already on full. That's the problem.'

'Oh wow. I just love these palms are they real? And those yuccas too. Must have cost you a pretty penny?'

'No, actually we got them for free! A garden centre near Hull was giving them away rather than see them die off when they had to shut at the start of the first phase of lock-down.'

'Do you watch that garden makeover programme with Alan Titchmarsh? You know, where you often see them craning trees into back gardens over the roof.'

'Yes, it's a favourite of mine. Why?'

'Well they sometimes tell you the cost breakdown of the project and I can tell you that if you had to buy those palms today they'd set you back over five hundred quid each. And the yuccas a couple of hundred each. You've got about three grand's worth of tropical vegetation in here. What sort of lighting effect did you want to try and create exactly?'

Millie told him roughly what she had in mind and then they were off.

'I'll be in touch. Thanks for the coffees.'

Bridlington beckoned.

26.

Dusk fell just after six o'clock. It wouldn't be long before the clocks went forward and the whole country could feel more optimistic. It was time for the switch-on for the new sign in darkness. The three youngsters all gathered outside in the drive while Dad stayed inside to throw the switch. It was like a miniature version of town centre Christmas lights being switched on by a celebrity.

'Get ready Dad -five-four-three-two-one Go!'

Three seconds of flickering later the new sign glowed like a radio-active isotope. It was truly the start of a new beginning. On the footpath outside an elderly couple were walking a dog – an even older Labrador by its slow speed. They couldn't help but notice the new sign with its emerald photons reflecting in the adjacent palm leaves.

'Hey-up. Look at that! Looks like its going to reopen soon. New name an'all. I wonder who's gorrit now? Can't be any worse than that t'other lot. Well dodgy if you ask me. What did happen to them anyway?' They shuffled on, the dog smelling something new to sniff a few yards further.

The next day brought truly unexpected news for the Fishburn family, the battered hospitality industry and indeed the whole nation. Government Ministers had assembled in the Downing Street briefing room and the attending Press Corps must have been given an advance tip-off of what was to follow. Nobody was sitting two metres apart, nobody was wearing one of those ghastly blue facemasks manufactured by the million in Asian sweatshops but absolutely everyone was wearing something in common – a smile. A hush descended on the huge room as no less than the Prime Minister himself strode purposefully to the lectern and twin microphones.

'Ladies and gentlemen here present and to the millions watching and listening around the United Kingdom, I bring you wonderful news. Our medical advisers have recommended that over the next few weeks all Covid-related restrictions will slowly be eased and by Easter will be dropped in their entirety The sacrifices have been huge and there is not a family in the land that has not suffered either painful bereavement or financial hardship, This is particularly true to those of you who work in the hospitality industry. Whether you are a bar-worker, waitress, cook or a hotelier or restaurateur, you have borne a huge burden for far too long. International travel will, I suspect, take many months to return to normal so it is therefore my dearest hope that British resorts will benefit in a way that we haven't seen since the end of the Second World War. I wish all of you many happy days besides the seaside as we all start to enjoy and appreciate what we have to offer on our own doorsteps. May I wish each and every one of you a Happy Holiday.'

In the Hotel Scarbados the mood was ecstatic. Pete went straight to the wall-mounted calendar in the kitchen and started to count the number of days to 'launch' as he put it.

'Right then, I make it sixteen days exactly. Two weeks on Friday, Good Friday, we can open.'

Mandy was not impressed.

'I thought Fridays were supposed to be unlucky for new ventures, ship launches and the like.'

Millie grabbed the moment.

'You're right, so let's officially open the evening before with a Welcome Buffet and invite as many people as we can. Yes? We can use the conservatory to lay out all the food and where folks can chat and mingle. Dave Gibson will have completed the new lighting by then won't he Dad?'

'I'll call him to make sure. Some of his ideas were just amazing. I've already sent photos of the outside of the hotel, including the new sign of course, to Katya. I did photos in the daylight and at night with the new sign looking amazing. Katya says she'll have basic outline of the website, a sort of proof if you like, ready by this evening. The conservatory pics can be added later – in fact at any time. So can anything else, that's the beauty of a website. You can't do that if we'd say advertised in a newspaper or holiday brochure. It's a whole new ballgame nowadays.'

'Haven't we missed something that's rather crucial to the whole business, Millie?'

'What's that, Dad?'

'Prices! What are our rates going to be?'

'Dad, the word is Tariffs in the hotel business. It's not a supermarket. We've all got to start not just using a new language but thinking in it too. Does everyone agree?'

Everyone smiled and nodded, except her mother. Mandy had gone into the lounge with a coffee and a newspaper, the Hull Daily Mail, before the Prime Minister had even finished his address to the nation. It was all more than a bit worrying.

With only just over a fortnight to go, it was like the start of an athletics event. The starting gun had finally been fired. Millie got out the file marked Business Plan that she had commenced all those months ago. It was putting on weight.

Soon she would have to start separate files for the Bank, the VAT. She delegated a lot to her father Peter but under her tutor Mr White's guidance she would look after the banking and tax affairs.

The new Alcohol Licence had been obtained and paid for relatively easily with Melanie's help. They made sure that non-residents were permitted too.That reminded her, that there was another person to invite to the Opening Night. She had already asked Mr White and his wife to attend and accommodation in the best guest room facing the park had been reserved for them. It was only the right thing to do. It wouldn't interfere with anything and in any event paying guests would not be booked in properly until the following day, Good Friday. It was time for a more serious chat with Jamie about the cooking arrangements. She was very careful not to let on that she and Samantha Lyon had not even met, let alone spoken. Tact was not normally her forté so she had to tread carefully.

'Jamie, let's me and you have chat on our own OK? Let's take a coffee into the conservatory shall we?'

'OK Sis, I haven't had much chance to catch you on your own. I want to tell you about this Scarborough TEC situation and what I might be doing.'

Millie played dumb. Before coffees had even been made the rattle of the letterbox opening and snapping shut under its strong springs brought Seb trotting to the front door with a bark and then another. Peter beat everyone to the door and was almost disappointed to note that the sole envelope on the mat was not what he'd been hoping for. Unbeknown to the rest of the family he'd invested all of his redundancy money from P & O into Premium Savings Bonds. This month was the first one he was eligible to win a prize but perhaps he was being a tad optimistic to think that Ernie was going to be so generous so quickly. He wasn't aware that it took a minimum of a month to get into the system.

'It's addressed to you, Jamie. It's franked Scarborough TEC. What's that all about?'

'Dad, I'll come clean. Grab a coffee and join me and Millie in the conservatory.'

Within two minutes the three of them were sat around an attractive rattan coffee table with an attractive glass top in the centre circle. It reflected the overhead light very well even before the imminent upgrade. Jamie deftly slit open the envelope. He knew roughly what its contents would say so he had no hesitation in reading it out word for word.

'Dear Jamie

I write following our recent meeting and discussions here in my office.

It is my pleasure to confirm that you are being offered a place on our new eight week Catering Course.

Please understand that this is NOT a formal qualification and is intended to assist the hospitality industry as it recovers from many months of hardship.

The course itself will commence on the first working day after all the restrictions have been lifted.

You should attend at ten o'clock prompt and classes will finish around four in the afternoon. This is to allow those of you already working, perhaps on split shifts, to work and study at the same time.

Later in the summer we will be offering two further specialist modules and you are invited to select ONE of them.

The choices are 'Beers, Wines & Spirits' Or Nutrition. This will allow every one of you to gain knowledge in either the hospitality industry or the care industry.

Places will be strictly limited so you must confirm your intentions as soon as possible. You do not have to confirm your choice of the extra module until the end of the main course.

Perhaps I ought to say that you can choose your pudding later!

With kind regards,

Samantha Lyon
Head of Department.

Jamie took a long slurp of his coffee and waited for his father's and sister's reactions. Dad was first.

'Well, I must say this is a total if pleasant surprise. What do you think Millie?'

'Come here Bro and give me a hug. What a star you are!' Dad hadn't finished.

'And I'll tell you now, you can leave all that nutrition nonsense to the Care Homes. Don't forget, I've been dealing with booze most of my working life. I'll teach you all I know before you've even started that module. Now I know what to buy you for your eighteenth birthday next month, son.'

'Let me guess – a combined corkscrew and bottle opener?' They all laughed.

'Not exactly but you're not far off.' The door suddenly clicked open. Was it Seb pushing his cold nose in? No, it was far worse. It was Mandy.

'I heard all that nonsense. Who on Earth do you think you are? Jamie bloody Oliver? So that's where you skived off to the other afternoon is it? You should go back to 'Ull, finish your 'A' levels and either get a proper job or go do a degree in something useful.' Jamie reacted instantly and for the first time in his life he cut the apron strings.

'Mam, you're wrong. Why would I want a degree in something I don't want to do and end up with a horrendous student loan to boot eh? Why?' But Mandy was back in Hull fish-wife mode.

'Have it your own way, all of you. Anyway, I'm going back to 'Ull for the Easter weekend. It's me sister Gwen's birthday on Easter Monday. Her sixty-fifth and we're all off to Willerby Manor for a nice lunch. Now, where's my Daily Mail.'

'Kids. I think we've got a problem with your Mam. She hasn't settled here at all has she? Any ideas what we can do? It's very upsetting.' All of a sudden he had pangs of guilt about his long-term dalliances in Belgium. Millie rescued his hurt with an even bigger hug than she had given her brother. And she didn't even know the rest. Not yet anyway. Jamie felt guilty too but for different reasons.

'I think the break will do her good, Dad. She'll come back a different person.' He was right there.

Right, you two. Let's tick off what's still left to do shall we?

'Jamie, how about this for an idea. Why don't you ask that Ms Lyon was it, to advise us on an Opening Night buffet? You never know, she might be quite helpful. In fact, I know, how about inviting her when you formally accept the place on the course?'

'That sounds great. In fact can you type me out a letter please? I'll sign it and take it up to the College on my bike. It's only fifteen minutes away.'

'Sure, but let's just tick off a few more boxes on this 'to do' list first shall we? Dad, have either you or Mum opened our account at the Cash & Carry yet? We'll need proper and regular supplies from now on. It's not just our own mouths to feed is it? For a start we'll need enough for thirty-two breakfasts a day, assuming maximum occupancy. We don't want to be caught with our pants down do we?'

'Right, Jamie, lets write and print out that letter now shall we? How do you want me to word it?'

'Not sure. You know English isn't my strong point, Sis. Can't you do it?'

'OK just this once but it'll cost you.'

'Yeah, like what?'

'Breakfast in bed on Easter Sunday.'

'You'll be lucky. With any luck I'll be too busy!'

'Go and get your bike kit on then. I'll only take me five minutes. And quite apart from learning English you're going to have to familiarise yourself with a smattering of French. Won't he Dad?'

'What for? Frog, you're kidding?'

'Jamie, French is the international language of food and drink. I'll draw up a list of words and phrases while you're delivering your acceptance letter.' She was already mentally concocting a list:

Cordon-bleu
Vin de table
Appellation controlleé
Bon appetit
Flambé
Potage du jour
Sommelier

It was going to be a much longer list, that's for sure. But by the time he even started the course he would already be streets ahead of the others in the class. She would 'make it so' as a Starship Commander was often fond of saying. A half an hour later and Jamie was on his bike. She had fifteen minutes to make the call.

'Hi Sam. Jamie's hand delivering his acceptance of a place on your short Course. He'll be there soon, assuming little or no traffic.'

'That's great news. Now, I've been thinking about your Opening Night. How about welcoming glasses of fizz as they arrive with a nice choice of canapés to suit every taste and palate. A simple but hot buffet might be along the lines of a vegetarian lasagne or beef stroganoff accompanied by either a ratatouille or a hot Mediterranean salad? The clocks might have gone forward by then but it will still be cool. Don't forget it's Scarborough, not Barbados!'

''Wonderful! I'm not sure that we'll be up to that level of expertise by then though.'

'You won't have to be. It'll be wonderful experience for my students already on the Advanced Diploma course. It'll be a piece of cake for them. And speaking of cake how about a nice fresh gâteaux to finish off with? We'd better finish this conversation now. I think I can hear Jamie's motorbike outside my office window.'

'OK, Sam, thanks again and speak soon.'

'You bet.'

Within a minute Millie added two more French words to her list – canapé and gâteaux. How could she possibly have forgotten?

27.

It was Maundy Thursday and the great day had arrived. They were all up and awake early and after a rushed minimalist breakfast that made even a continental breakfast look 'over the top' they set to work making sure that every thing was orderly and ship-shape. Even Mandy, who's mind was already on her imminent trip to Hull, got stuck in.

'We want the place to look spick and span for all our visitors this evening. First impressions always count.'

Suddenly she morphed into a woman possessed.

Millie, I said I wanted a nice bouquet of flowers in the hall. Where are they? Do I have to remind you about everything? Lilies. Tiger if you can get them, Oriental if you can't.

'Lucy, never mind taking the dog out for a walk. Have you vacuumed the dining room – and the lounge? No. Now please.'

The mere fact that she called Seb 'the dog' emphasised her annoyance.

'And where's Jamie bloody Oliver when you want him? If he's out on his damned bike again I'll play war with him.' Pete arrived on the scene.

'Ah, there you are. Are you taking me to the railway station later? My train's at four o'clock and I don't want to be late. My case is in the hall. Put in the back of the car now then it's done isn't it?'

'What? I thought you were going tomorrow, not today.'

'On Good Friday? What planet do you live on? If they're not on holiday they're on strike.'

'OK, Mandy. Anything you say. We'll leave here at three forty-five. OK?'

'No, half past three to be on the safe side. The traffic out there is terrible apparently. Put the radio on.'

'BBC Radio York traffic news – the latest from Bek Homer live, on the ground in Scarborough.

Good morning, residents and visitors alike please take note. All main roads to the coast are exceptionally busy. North Yorkshire Police report that traffic on the A64 from York and Leeds is moving only slowly. The A165 from Hull is almost as bad and north of Bridlington it's almost stationary. There is little traffic on the A171, the Whitby Road. Drivers should allow three hours from York to Scarborough. And now back to the studio. Ellie.'

'You see, I told you. So where is Jamie anyway?'

'He's in the shed doing a bit of carpentry. He's been at it for a few days now.'

'At what? Carpentry? I've never seen him with anything but a set of bike spanners. What's he playing at?'

'I think he'd like to show you himself. Just let him get on with it OK?' Mandy shrugged her shoulders and sighed. She was secretly pleased that she would be absent for the evening's events. Far too many people and far too much noise.

An hour later and Jamie emerged from the shed with his masterpiece. Before the dining room had received its upgrade he had removed a radiator shelf about a yard long, six inches wide and at least an inch thick. It was a bit 'distressed' as the woodwork purists would put it but it looked like oak to him, not that he was an expert. He had stripped it down to remove what looked like the remnants of a shellac or varnish. The heat from the radiator had affected it somewhat and he couldn't help but wonder how long it had been there. If only he knew. It would be some time before he found out. Days earlier he had rubbed the 'plank' down with wire wool to the bare wood and applied a generous amount of a stain from a tin that he had found in the shed. The label "dark oak" was the only legible lettering. Three coats on three consecutive days were followed by several hours of hand polishing. Three brass instruments were screwed into place at equidistant intervals. He walked into the hall holding his finished work with both hands in front of him like he'd just caught a prize-winning salmon.

'Well, folks. This is my contribution to the hall décor. Not bad eh?' Peter and Mandy were blown away. It looked like something from the bridge of the Queen Mary,

'Well say something for goodness sake. What do you think?'

Peter did a double take. In between two identical brass ship's clocks was the barometer that his former mistress had given him. A small brass tag on the clock to the left read 'Barbados' and one under the other 'Scarborough.'

'You know those fancy intercontinental hotels in London like the Ritz? They always have a string of clocks from left to right along the time zones from Los Angeles to New York to London to Tokyo don't they? Well in view of our name the Hotel Scarbados, we've got Barbados Time and Scarborough Time. Barbados is four hours behind us so I've set them accordingly. What d'ya think?'

Pete blinked and just hoped that nobody asked too many questions about the SVG tag under the barometer. He threw in a question to divert any enquiries on the barometric front.

'Just out of interest where did you get the two clocks and those lovely brass corners from? It all looks very expensive.'

'Well the marine clocks I got from the same company in London as made the barometer – Comitti. Their website is amazing. And the smart brass corners I found in a drawer in the shed not far from the tin of oak stain. Smart aren't they? They really set it off. According to the small plastic bag it was originally an eight-pack. You know, the sort of handy things they sell in blister packs like picture hooks and brass screws.'

To Peter's immense relief no more was said about the barometer. Mandy knew she had to say something.

'It's beautiful, darling, just beautiful. And I thought you were out skiving on your bike. I'm so sorry. Come her give your Mam a hug.'

Twenty minutes later and the clock and barometer combination was perfectly in place directly above the small but attractive reception desk. It would impress any first time visitor who, at first glance, might think that they were either living a life on the ocean wave or in the Caribbean drinking rum punches as the sun set behind the palm-lined beach. That, of course, was exactly what it was supposed to do.

By lunchtime the girls had vacuumed the entire downstairs and it looked like a new pin. The conservatory had a laminate flooring to make cleaning easier but it was given a quick once-over with the new electric polisher to give it that Mr Sheen glow and pleasant aroma. A final test was made of the new overhead brass fans and the revolutionary hi-tech lighting system that Dave Gibson had installed only the day before. It was something else and was more of a projector than a lighting system. A black gizmo discretely tucked into a corner of the ceiling could radiate any chosen light, or combination of lights, onto any part of the whole room. If you wanted a pale yellow Arabian style sunset, you've got it. If you wanted a turquoise blue water to appear behind the strategically placed palms and yuccas, you've got it. It was limited only by your imagination and your dexterity with the remote control almost identical to that of a domestic TV. Boy, were they going to have fun with this on special events nights – and they hadn't even opened yet.

At three-thirty prompt Peter took his wife to the railway station. They travelled in almost total silence. The peck on the cheek to her husband after he had unloaded her somewhat heavy case was perfunctory.

'Bye love, and I hope everything goes well tonight.' She meant it too. She just didn't want to take part.

An hour later from the train window she could see the spire of Beverley Minster looming in the fading light. Soon she would be home, her home – 'Ull.'

28.

Back from the railway station around four-thirty, Peter was in a mood the like of which he had never known before. Today was the real start of a new life. Would the business work? A year ago he was heading for redundancy and personal oblivion but here he was now, joint owner of an old but newly refurbished hotel in England's oldest tourist resort. For over two centuries 'Scardeburg' had been providing the healing Spa waters to thousands of visitors. Like every resort in the land it had lost its glitter as millions of Brits had deserted their homeland for holidays in the sun but the unprecedented events of the last year or more had changed all that. The opportunities ahead for his family were immense but the day was tinged with sadness. Today, of all days, his wife of two decades had decided to stay away. It hurt. Pulling himself out of his temporary melancholy he went straight upstairs to smarten himself up. It wouldn't be long before people started to arrive.

First to arrive were Mr & Mrs Clive White who had driven from Cottingham, a large village-like satellite of Hull. Millie was so pleased they had accepted her invitation. Without his experience and guidance where would they be? Certainly not where they are now, that's for sure. The business account at the Blackbird Bank, opened on his recommendation, had yet to receive its first credit and although this weekend was very much a promotion exercise the sincere hope was that at least a few rooms would be let to get the ball rolling. The Whites parked in one of the empty slots in the car park at the rear. Removing small overnight cases from the boot they were unsure whether to enter via the conservatory door which was slightly ajar or walk round to the front. They decided on the front and a minute later entered the hall. Young Jamie was behind the reception desk.

'Good afternoon, or is it good evening? And a very warm welcome to the Hotel Scarbados. You must be Mr & Mrs White. May I take your coats and luggage for you?' Now he knew what Samantha Lyon had impressed upon him the first time he had entered her office.

'Thank you. You must be Jamie. Where's Millie?' He didn't have long to wait. About five seconds in fact. She floated down the last six steps of the broad staircase as if they weren't there. She wore a dark green dress of below the knee length with her auburn hair tied back with a pearly choker with a single string of pearls that had belonged to Peter's mother. A touch of rouge to her already freckled complexion added to her glowing persona.

'Mr White! And this must be Mrs White! Hello and welcome …'

'Please, it's Clive and this is the long-suffering Linda.'

'Isn't it strange? We've known each other for almost a year and have seen each other scores of times but only via Zoom. A head and shoulders relationship, if you like.'

'Did you think the rest of me would look like, a plump retired bank manager like Captain Mainwaring in Dad's Army? Ha ha!'

'No, not at all, you look quite fit in fact. Lucky you, Linda. Keep him on his toes!' She had a sense of humour.

'They say that if your name's Linda you have to be sixty-five plus as there aren't any girls called Linda these days – or even Lynda with a letter y – the posh version. My mother let me down.'

'Oh I don't know, there's Linda Carter, Wonderwoman!' They all laughed.

'Let me show you to your room. Jamie will take your cases upstairs I'm sure.'

She turned to face the reception desk. He'd already performed the task. He was learning. They all were. Five minutes later they came back downstairs.

'Come on then, Millie, give us the guided tour. Linda's very nosey and can't wait to see what you've done here.'

'No problem. Let's do the lounge, the dining room and then the conservatory which is our trademark I guess. Hopefully my sister Lucy has already left a pot of tea and biscuits for you in the lounge.'

A short time later Samantha Lyon arrived with two of her students, one male one female, attired in splendid maroon waistcoats emblazoned with a gold STEC logo. Talk about smart! The driver of the smallish white van outside started unloading trays of finger food – canapés, canapés and even more canapés – all wrapped in protective clingfilm. Fifteen minutes later and the conservatory resembled one of those temporary hospitality tents that you see at some sporting events like horse races and cricket matches. All they needed now was the guests to arrive. To say that this was an unknown quantity was a gross understatement. Lots of invitations had been sent out, some in the post but most by email. The relaxation of the Covid rules had been so recent that things really were still nowhere near normal. All they could do was to 'go for it' and hope for the best.

Jamie and Lucy had seemingly vanished into thin air but when they suddenly reappeared down the main staircase Millie had to do a double take. They were both wearing immaculately fitted tailored waistcoats in dark green and showing off a shiny gold logo – hotel SCARBADOS – in the same style as the new sign on the front of the hotel. Millie was stunned.

'Oh my God, where did they come from?' Samantha just smiled.

'I got the tailor who does our college garb to knock four up for you, two each. One soup spill and it's in the wash. You always need back-up. It's a little gift from the college to thank you for the invitation tonight. And in any event we'll get a little publicity for this tonight. I hope you don't mind but I've put a little notice on the main table where the Gâteaux is being displayed. It just says 'Refreshments provided by Scarborough TEC Faculty of Catering' I know it sounds a bit pompous but I'm keen to promote the College and what it can do for the local hospitality industry. Right now it needs all the help it can get. Lots of small businesses have had to close, never to return.'

'That's no problem at all, Sam. And just look at that beautiful Gâteaux. It looks almost tropical with that amount of fruit on that sea of cream. Where on Earth did you get that many different kinds at this time of year?'

'Millie, in this trade it's who you know not what you know, as you are about to find out.'

A corpulent gentleman in his late sixties swaggered into the conservatory with a glass of Prosecco in each hand. Perhaps one was for his wife. Wrong, he just liked his drink and was taking full advantage of the free hospitality.

'Ah, there you are Samantha. Thanks awfully for the invitation. And who's this gorgeous young lady here may I ask.' Millie was a little miffed but hid her feelings for the moment.

'Millie, this is Miles Carter. He's the Treasurer of Scarborough Cricket Club. Miles, this is Millie Fishburn, eldest daughter of the proprietors.' Instantly he morphed into a gentleman and placed the flute in his right hand on the nearest table so he could shake hands.

'Delighted, delighted.'

He was about to say 'do you come here often?' but checked himself at the last second.

'What a delightful job you've made of the refurb if I may say so. It's a few years since I was last in this hotel but it was called something else then. Buggered if I can remember.'

'The Wendover, Mr Carter, the Wendover. We changed the name as soon as we could. You know, a new start and all that.'

'I think your new name is just great. It's got a certain zing to it hasn't it? Are any of your family cricket fans by any chance?'

'Well my Grandad used to watch a team in Hull called Hull Zambezi or something like that anyway.'

'I think you mean Hull Zingari – goodness knows where that name comes from. They used to come and play in Scarborough when we both played in the same league. And your father, does he watch cricket at all?' They hadn't noticed that Peter was only a few feet away chatting to a lady from the Scarborough Hoteliers Association. He excused himself and walked towards Mr Carter and Millie.

'I overheard you. Hello, I'm Peter Fishburn, pleased to meet you Mr Carter.'

'Please, it's Miles. Look it's awfully nice to meet you and to have a butchers at the Hotel but I might just have a small business proposition for you. Er, any chance of another glass of this excellent fizzy vino?' The dutiful Jamie was already poised behind him with a recently opened fresh bottle.

'Actually, Sir, it's a Castellore Organico from north-eastern Italy. A slightly almond bouquet on the nose but a delightful finish I think. Do try it with a gravadlax canapé or two. Ah here comes Lily, one of my soon to be fellow students, with a nice selection. Then try the Caspian caviare on the French toast with organic vinaigrette. It's wonderful.' Millie didn't know whether to laugh or cry. He hadn't even started the course yet. Where on Earth did he get all that blurb from?

The evening went down superbly and by about nine o'clock the last of the guests drifted away. The four of them plus Clive and Linda White reclined in the lounge with coffee and Baileys and several trays of left-over canapés. It wasn't an inquest but more of a review of what they'd done right and what they'd done wrong. Clive opened the batting.

'Look, I've been to umpteen of these sorts of Welcome Evenings and I can tell you it's not an exact science. The important thing is that everybody seemed to enjoy themselves and everyone was very complimentary. Jamie, how many of the Hotel's business cards were taken?'

'Eighty-two. There are eighteen left of the one hundred I left out on the reception desk. That was a brilliant idea of yours.'

'Good. I counted forty people here this evening which necessarily means that many folks took two or more. That's important as it usually means they'll get passed on. It's one step at a time. Now, time to retire I think. Well done everybody.'

The next morning they all had breakfast together and Jamie offered them a choice of anything from his new 'pilot' menu. Nobody chose the kedgeree, thank goodness, Shortly after ten the Whites got ready to leave for the drive back to Cottingham. The traffic was still forecast to be heavy as thousands headed for the coast but fortunately they were headed in the opposite direction this time. Clive White had not quite finished his comments.

'Just one last question if I may before we set off. Why's your dog always got such a muddy nose?'

Lucy was the first to react.

'Oh Sebbie, don't tell me you've been digging again. What is it with you anyway? Here, have a leftover cocktail sausage. Good boy.'

29.

'So, Dad. What exactly did that Mr Carter from the Cricket Club actually want, apart from another drink?'

'Ha, yes you could tell he liked a tipple or two and I noticed he had an extra helping of that superb gâteaux. Maybe that could be our trademark dessert – the Scarbados Gâteaux – something for you to think about maybe, Jamie?' Before he could even answer Millie's mobile did a double 'ping' in her jeans back pocket,

'Great news it's a message from Katya. Our website's ready to go live but she wants us to approve it first. She's sent me the link. Now let's see, where's my laptop? Oh yes I remember now. It's behind reception. We'll need a proper desk-top PC when we're functioning properly. I'll check out suitable models on line after this weekend. Peter just sighed and looked skywards. Why couldn't people just go to a proper shop any more? No wonder small businesses were going bust left, right and centre. Two minutes later and Millie returned with the laptop already displaying the hotelscarbados.com website.

'Oh wow! Doesn't it look great? Look Dad, there's you talking to that Mr Carter. Thank goodness he's only got a glass in one hand. It would have looked awful if he'd …'

'What?! But that was only last night so how come …'

'Dad, I took quite a few pics last night and I emailed a selection of them to Katya before I even went to bed. That's how things are done these days. It's so quick. Instant marketing. Look, there's another one of Jamie and Lucy in their new waistcoats. Smart or what?'

'Well, I still think that your Mum's idea of putting a small ad in the Hull Daily Mail might not be a bad idea. We all know it's her favourite paper.'

'Dad, that's why it's called that – it's a daily paper. Twenty four hours later and it's either in the bin or being used to wrap up cod and chips. Get real. I'll tell you what though, I might ask them if they're interested in doing an advertorial.'

'An adver what?'

'An advertorial. It's quite the thing these days. It's a cross between an advertisement and an editorial. They do a feature on us and slot it in on a day when there's little news to report. It fills a page for them and gives us some publicity. I'll give them a call next week when the features editor is back at work after the Easter break OK? Leave it with me. By the way you still haven't answered my question?'

'What question was that?'

'What did Mr Carter want? He was talking to you for ages. Maybe it was just the drink talking, after all he had plenty.'

'No you're wrong there. It was serious stuff and potentially very lucrative for us. It concerns having some sort of a tie-up with the Cricket Club itself.'

'Really, in what way?'

'Well it was very noisy as you know with so many folks gabbling at the same time. From what I gather though, the Club is recruiting some junior players from overseas for the forthcoming summer season and is looking for a deal on accommodation for them. He asked if we'd like to chat to him again in the Club's offices one day next week. He gave me his card with a view to my calling him to arrange a suitable day and time. What do you think, Millie? Jamie, Lucy, what do you two think?'

Millie heard all and said nowt, as they say in Yorkshire and that applies to every Riding, not just the North and East varieties. If they wanted something for nothing they were in for a surprise. And if they wanted something cheap then there had to be a quid pro quo.

'OK Dad, you and Jamie go and meet him and see what the score is – excuse the pun. You never know. Anyway, are we all agreed that our website can go out as it is now? Hands up.'

Three hands were raised. She was interrupted by the front door bell ringing. Jamiee did the honours and attended. A smart chap in his early forties had already walked into the hall towards the Reception desk.

'Yes, Sir, can I help you?'

'Good morning, I hope so. We're in a bit of a pickle. I'm with three mates, that's our 4x4 outside. We've just blocked your drive I hope you don't mind but we couldn't see the remotest possibility of parking within half a mile. I have never seen Scarborough so crowded.'

'No worries, Sir. How can we assist?'

'We need accommodation for three nights, for all four of us. We had reservations at the Lancelot Guest House up near the golf club. When we got there an hour ago they told us that they were very sorry but due to a computer error they had double booked some rooms including the two twin rooms we had reserved. We've driven round and round asking umpteen establishments but everywhere seems to be overflowing. As it happens the last place we called at, somewhere near a bowling centre, was owned by a lady from a Hotel Association or something like that anyway. She gave us one of your cards and said try them, So here we are. Here's the card – look.'

He pulled it out from the breast pocket of his blue denim shirt with a golf club logo embossed on it.

Jamie knew full well that thus far the Hotel was still empty but he played it cool.

'I'll just check for you. I can give you four double rooms for three nights with no single person supplements – on this occasion only mind you.'

'Wow how come? I thought you'd be heaving. How long have you been open if you don't mind me asking?'

'We took over just before Christmas from the old owners but because of the Covid restrictions only just being lifted, this is actually our very first day of trading. You guys are our very first customers. May I bid you a very warm welcome to the Hotel Scarbados!'

'You can and you may, young man. I must say I just love that waistcoat. Can we park properly, round the back presumably?'

'Yes of course. If you unload your cases now by the front door I'll arrange to take them to your rooms and I'll get the keys for you.'

'Proper keys eh? I like a proper key – none of those plastic things with a magnetic strip on that always seem to go wrong at the most inconvenient time. Just before lock-down we were playing in a knock-out foursome competition at a place called Forest Pines. Do you know it?'

'No, Sir, I don't. We're actually not from round here. We're originally from Hull.'

'Ah well, then if you go over the Humber Bridge and head towards Sunny Scunny it's not far from there. One of our keys failed completely just after midnight and with no staff on duty four of us had to bunk up in one twin room. We were knackered the next morning and lost the semi-final by a country mile. Anyway, I'll get the luggage out and put the motor round the back. Cheers.... sorry what is your name?'

'Jamie, Jamie Fishburn. I'll come and give you a hand.' Jamie made a mental note to ask Millie about some nice shiny brass name badges made for all of them. No doubt Lucy would ask if Seb could have one too. He would also remind her to have Seb's chip renewed with his new address and contact details.

Ten minutes later the four golfers were back in the lobby, their cases safely tucked upstairs.

'Hi again Jamie, we're not playing our first game until three o'clock this afternoon up at the North Cliff course. Can you tell us where's good near here to get a snack – you know a sandwich or something?'

'Sure, just keeping walking towards the sea past those two smart blocks of flats and you'll come across two or three cafés. Three o'clock did you say? You'd best look smart then. It's getting dark just after six. I know this because our hotel sign is light-sensitive and came on just as the news was on TV last night. By the way, have you made any arrangements for an evening meal? I'd normally recommend Clarkson's Cuisine near the park entrance but I understand it's fully booked and has been for two weeks. Folks are going mad, like they've been let out of prison.'

'Oh crikey. Got any ideas?'

'Yes, Jamie's Caff! I can knock you up four portions of Beef Strogg followed by a tropical fruit gâteaux. Will that do you?'

'Deal!'

Jamie had six hours to get the recipe. He didn't tell them it was yesterday's leftover gâteaux.

The team of four had cheese and pickle sandwiches and vegetable soup for lunch. They were all in a buoyant mood. It was just Day One of proper trading, four rooms were already let out for the next three nights and at long last after many trials and tribulations they were finally in business. Millie was particularly up-beat.

'Yes, another one of Clive's ideas has paid off already. The business cards I mean. I got a small batch of two hundred and fifty from a company online and ….'

'Here we go again. For God's sake let's get a good local firm to design some new ones from scratch. You can get them where the logo is embossed with a thermal heat process and boy do they look posh or what?'

'OK Dad, just for once you might be right. I'll check it out next week. Let's hope those we've got left last us until then. Whatever though it's been a cute investment already. If that lady from the Hotels Association hadn't picked up a card and maybe a spare, this golfing guy wouldn't even know we existed now would he? It's a form of networking I suppose. Jamie, when these guys check out on Monday let's make sure they've each got a couple to take home.' Jamie had a better idea.

'No let's give 'em at least six each. Those posh golf clubs sometimes have hundreds of members. If those guys sing our praises we could do very well from personal recommendations. Don't they say that 'word of mouth' is the best form of advertising?'

Millie smiled the biggest smile Pete could ever remember. He was so chuffed. His three kids were maturing into the business at an almost alarming rate. His happiness was tempered only by the fact that his wife Mandy wasn't taking part. Perhaps the break in Hull would do her good. Some hope. Last night she had scooped the one thousand pound Easter Prize at MECCA Bingo and if anything felt even more at home in 'Ull.

30.

The long weekend passed very quickly. Apart from the four golfers, three other couples literally rang the bell and asked if there were any vacancies.

'It would help if you had a "Vacancies" or "No Vacancies" sign in the window, tha' knows, my dear' remarked one lady trying to be helpful. We just assumed you were full, you know, with Scarborough being so busy. We just thought we'd try on the off chance. We were on the point of giving up and driving back to Skipton to be honest.

Jamie was on desk duty at the time and took the remark as well intended.

'Thank you, Madam. I'll take that on board, as it were. We've only just moved here from Hull and only opened our doors on Friday. Are you regular visitors to Scarborough may I ask?'

'Oh yes, we are aren't we Fred? Fred?! He never wears his hearing aids. Drives me mad, he does.'

'My Grandad was the same. Let me help you get the bags in from the car.'

'I'll sign us both in. He never remembers his reading glasses either. Now, where's the Register?'

Jamie gulped. They hadn't even got one. How on earth did they forget to purchase that most fundamental part of the business? Come to think of it they hadn't even seen an old one left behind by the previous owners. He made a mental note to tell his Dad and Millie. Perhaps they could acquire one quickly via a specialist online supplier?

'We'll deal with the Register formalities later Mrs er ….'

'Coates, Fred and Babs Coates. And you are who, young man?'

'Jamie Fishburn, It's my Mam and Dad's hotel but we run it as a family. I have two sisters … and a dog called Seb.'

'Oh that's nice. We much prefer to stay in smaller family-run hotels when we come to Scarborough. We've left our doggie in kennels for a few days. Not that we like doing it but most places don't allow dogs do they? They're throwing business away if you ask me.'

'So, if you don't mind my asking, where do you normally stay? You're obviously regular visitors to the town.'

'We used to stay at a place called The Cricketers up on North Marine Road, right opposite the cricket ground itself. We're big fans. Now that the Covid nonsense is over we'll be resuming our regular trips here won't we Fred? I said won't we Fred?'

But Fred wasn't paying the slightest bit of attention to her indoors. He was staring up at the double clock and barometer set on the wall behind the reception desk and was miles away. Four thousand miles in fact.

'Aye. I remember when I was a lad seeing Sobers playing here for a West Indies match. He was from Barbados. The world's best all-rounder according to most folks.'

'I wouldn't disagree with that statement.' Peter had arrived on the scene.

'Peter Fishburn, Jamie's dad. 'Ow do? Are you being looked after?'

'Eh? You what?' Mrs Coates intervened.

'He's as deaf as a post without his hearing aids. I hope he's remembered to pack them. He drives me mad. And yes, thank you, we are being well looked after. I was just saying that we have to leave our dog in kennels these days.'

'Well I can tell you that following pressure from my youngest daughter, Lucy, we might soon be able to announce that we'll be a dog-friendly hotel before the real season gets under-way. We'll just put a few adaptations into place first and we'll let you know.

'That's wonderful news. We'll get booked in before we leave. Won't we Fred? I said won't we Fred?'

The Coates's went to their room, this one overlooking the back and the long garden. Pete made another mental note to ask them about the Cricket Club. Did they know any other cricket fans from out of town? He would chat to them again, perhaps after the evening meal. Tonight's 'dish of the day' was a beef bourguignon served with saffron rice followed by the "Hotel Scarbados Gâteaux" as there was still half a square metre of it left in the fridge. Only now did Jamie realise that was why Samantha Lyon had told him to aim for seven signature dishes. The likelihood of any guest staying more than a week were slim. Five more dishes to learn. Five more to go, let's hope there's nothing too tricky to master before he completes the crash course which he now knew was starting in just a few days time.

The Coates's were chilling in the lounge after dinner with a cup of tea and a shortbread and Pete was keen to find out a little more about their links to the Cricket Club.

'So, you are regular visitors but how long have you been coming here Babs?'

'Must be over forty years now. We're Life Members of the Club and between me and thee we're also major donors to the Club. Consequently at the annual Festival in September we always get invited into the President's tent for a fancy lunch, you know, one of those big fancy marquees with flags on the top. It's not what it used to be years ago. Times change don't they?'

'Well you might like to know that the Club Treasurer, a chap called Miles Carter, was a guest here at our Open Evening last Friday. He said he had a proposition to put to me but we had to leave it for a while as it was so busy and I was mingling with folks anyway. He asked me to give him a call after the weekend.'

'Miles? We've known Miles for years! It's him we send our extra donations to before the start of every season. You wait till I see him. I'll tell him to treat you right, don't you worry.'

'Any idea what might be on his mind?'

'Well like everywhere else the Club will have had a poor time over the epidemic and lock-down. Crazy wasn't it? Beaches thronged with folks but nobody could go to a cricket match or a football match. Barmy if you ask me. Let me know how you get on with him won't you? And before I forget, there are four other couples who live near us in Carleton in Craven and we've often thought about arranging a small mini-bus to bring us all over together. It would be a lot easier if we all stayed at the same spot. Maybe you could give us a Group rate? We'd also need a packed lunch to take to the cricket on most days. The others would anyway as they're not donors but keep that to yourself. Well, what do you reckon? Yay or nay?'

Peter's brain was buzzing. Hadn't any other hotels thought about similar arrangements before?

'Bab's, I'm sure we can come to some suitable deal for you. Let me talk to Millie, she's our in-house accountant. You're here until Monday aren't you. I'll get back to you, I promise.'

Pete went into the drawer behind the reception desk to check that Miles Carter's business card was where he'd put it. Thankfully it was. The four golfers had gone 'out for a stroll' after dinner, probably in search of a nineteenth hole despite the fact that the hotel Bar was available. They probably needed the fresh air and to walk off the heavy meal. Returning just after ten o'clock they looked 'half-cut' and had obviously found a twentieth hole as well, never mind a nineteenth.

'Goodnight lads. And don't forget to put your watches forward an hour tonight. British Summer Time starts at midnight.'

He had genuinely forgotten to remind the Coates's – not that Fred would have heard him anyway. Forgetting to change the time in either Scarborough or Barbados, he locked the front door and turned out all the lights. That is all the lights except one – the new one over the front door. Just before midnight he was awoken by the bell ringing. He donned a dressing gown, flew downstairs still half-asleep and turned the double Yale lock. Two young men in their twenties without any luggage whatsoever looked slightly sheepish and one of them spoke, albeit slightly hesitatingly.

'Hi, are Marina or Katerina working tonight?'

'What?'

'You know, those two lasses from Romania. If not, then Olga or ...'

'Just bugger off! It's not that kind of place any-more.'

'Sorry mate. We noticed the light was still on and we used to pop in a lot whenever we were in town. Any idea where they are now? Absolute crackers they were and only fifty Euros a trick ...'

'Like I said, bugger off. Good night gentlemen.'

31.

On the Monday morning, Easter Monday, the Coates couple prepared to leave after a leisurely breakfast. They were about to check out and Millie was on the reception desk to finalise the bill.

'We've had a lovely stay haven't we Fred? I said haven't we Fred? I give up, daft as a brush as well as deaf as a post. And we'll be in touch again soon when we get the Cricket Club fixture list for the forthcoming season.'

'Thank you, Mrs Coates er Babs. And next time we'll make sure we have a proper Hotel register for you to sign! So many things to remember. Mum wouldn't have forgotten that. We're looking forward to her coming back on the train this afternoon. We're just waiting for a text or a call to tell us what time her train's arriving.'

'Such a shame her sister's not well. By the way if you've been wondering why we've been down late for breakfast the last couple of days it's because we didn't move our clocks and watches forward. It looks like you you didn't either by the look of those smart clocks up there.' Millie gulped.

'You just wait till I see Jamie. He did a wonderful job of putting it together but if the clocks aren't right it defeats the object.' Fred suddenly woke up.

'I'll tell you what he's done. He's moved the Barbados clock forward an hour but not the Scarborough clock. Look! There's always four hours difference between the two, not three hours.'

'Well spotted Mr Coates. But how did you know that exactly?'

'Because when England play Test Matches in Bridgetown, Barbados I always listen to it live on BBC Radio, you know, the ball by ball commentary.'

'So that's why you were often late to bed!'

Millie thought that maybe Fred wasn't as daft as his wife made out. A case of 'selective hearing' maybe?

'Here comes Jamie with your bags now. Would you like to bring your car to the front of the drive and Jamie'll pop them into the boot for you? Hopefully now that Covid is over the backlog in driving tests will be eroded , who knows, the next time you come here Jamie will be able to bring your car to the front door himself. You know, like they do in the movies at those posh hotels in London and Los Angeles.'

'You've been watching too much of that film called Pretty Woman, Millie. Mind you it's one of my favourites too. The best bit was when Julia Roberts tried eating those escargots – 'slippy little suckers' – remember that?'

'I do! Don't worry I can't see Jamie ever putting escargots on the menu, even when he's finished his course at Scarborough TEC.' Jamie actually overheard them but said nothing.

'Oh yes, one last favour please? When you get home can you put a review on Trip Adviser and Trust Pilot for us please? You know on the internet.'

'Of course we will, love, and if we get stuck then one of our neighbour's kids will help us out. T'internet's still a bit of a mystery to us, isn't it Fred. I said isn't it Fred?'

But Fred was already in the car fiddling with the clock which was still on Greenwich Mean Time. He was finding it tough and was mumbling to himself as to why car clocks were always so hard to alter. He wasn't alone. Millions of folks shared the same opinion. Sod it, he thought. It can jolly well stay on proper British Time.

'I say, Fred, you haven't changed the clock in the car. Look sharp.' Fred didn't hear her.

Before leaving Babs had made a request of them in return for a favourable Review.

'Next time can we please have a room facing the front and the park and not the rear and the garden?No offence, but that dog of yours woke me up every morning barking away under that tree as soon as it was light. Fred didn't hear of course.'

That it was a complaint as well as a request started to worry Millie. The whole notion of turning the Hotel Scarbados into a pooch-friendly 'kennel by the sea' didn't meet with her liking one bit. Was Lucy going to do all the dog-walking or what? She would talk to her Dad about in when Lucy took Seb out after lunch. Several bookings came in that morning, all by telephone. They had obtained a new land-line number and put it on the website which was just as well in view of what they had learned about the shady side of the Hotel's previous history. There had been a few more dubious door-knockers over the weekend. She tried not to think about it. Hopefully within a few days the bookings would start to come in via email and looking ahead prospective customers would be able to book totally on-line once the system was set up. The website was looking great and she must remember to invite Katya up for a "freebie weekend" as a thank you. Katya's input was innovative and starting to bear fruit but she had kept that from the rest of the family for the time being. In a couple of days time her Business and Accounting course would recommence after the Easter break and Jamie's crash catering course was starting tomorrow. They might have to start seriously considering hiring some local part-time staff, particularly on the housekeeping side. It had been intended that Mandy would assume the role of 'Housekeeper' but as the occupancy rate slowly increased the current "team of four" started to creak. The golfing guys had left that morning too, each with a few extra business cards. They were playing the last game of their little holiday at Ganton golf course just off the A64 on the way back to Leeds. Unbeknown to Millie one of them had already sent an email via his mobile phone to the Secretary of their own Club recommending the Hotel Scarbados. The last words simply said: 'Any members looking for a quick break try the Hotel Scarbados near Peasholm Park. Just opened. Only a mile away from North Cliff course. Good grub and it's LICENSED.'

Shortly after lunch Lucy grabbed Seb's lead. Normally eager to walk to Whitby and back whatever the weather, for the first time ever he didn't want to move a yard.

'What's up Sebbie? You're limping. Let me take a look. Oh my God, he's got a nasty splinter in his right front paw. Look! It's awful. No wonder he doesn't want to walk anywhere. It's too painful for him. Poor Sebbie. We'll have to take him to a vet as soon as possible. Jamie, can you pop next door and ask Garry if he can recommend a vet. Quickly please. I don't like the look of this at all. Go on quickly!'

Garry Ritson, bless him, was there in less than two minutes. He'd done a lot of voluntary work helping to train dog-handlers with North Yorkshire Police and he'd become a bit of a 'first responder' for dogs injured in training exercises. Lucy was in tears.

'It's Easter Monday and there won't be any vets available will there Mr Ritson?'

Garry was un-fazed. As I've said many times young Lucy, it's who you know not what you know. Now, where's my mobile?'

He pressed a few buttons and the speed dial soon reached its target.'

'Andrew Wilson, veterinary surgeon can I ...'

'Andrew, it's Garry. Bit of an emergency mate – my new neighbour's dog, a four year old Labradoodle.'

'What's up? Poisoning? It's all that anti-rodent stuff these days.'

'No. Somehow this dog has a large wooden splinter in its right front paw – not sure how yet.'

'Has it been on the beach today? Lots of strange driftwood about these days. Put your mobile on speaker, Garry.'

'Hello, I'm Lucy. He's my doggie really is Sebbie. Can you help please?'

'OK Lucy, did you hear that last bit? Has Sebbie been on the beach?'

'No, he's only been in the garden today.'

'Garry, as you know its a Bank Holiday so no other staff are around. Bring the dog to the surgery and I'll meet you both there in twenty minutes OK? Good job I'm not out walking or playing golf or whatever. See you there.'

Garry went and got his car then he and Lucy lifted Seb gently onto the back seat which was already covered in doggie blankets. Mercifully traffic was light and they were there in fifteen minutes. Andrew Wilson's 4 x4 Range Rover pulled in shortly after they did. It was covered in mud as usual. He was frequently called out to farms in the area and the lambing season was barely over.

'Right, you two. Give me two minutes to unlock then bring him into the treatment room.'

Garry carried Seb like he was holding a new born baby. Seb's twenty kilos was only half the weight of the numerous German Shepherds he'd brought in over the years following accidents out in the field. Andrew Wilson commenced his examination.

'Wow, that's a belter that one is! Never seen 'owt quite like it. Normally it's an old rose briar or a hawthorn twig. Right, it's got to come out but I'll have to locally anaesthetise him first. No other staff are on duty so. Lucy, I want you to help me please. Let's go and scrub up. Garry can stay with Sebbie can't you, Garry? Right let's get on with it then.'

Thirty minutes later and Seb's paw was dressed in a light bandage with a doggie shoe. He was more than a little jaded but his tail did a little wag seemingly in appreciation.

'Lucy, no long walkies for a few days, just around the garden OK? Here's the offending article for you to keep as a souvenir. Not nice is it? I want you to take a look in the garden and see if you can find anything that matches it. If you find anything remove it straight away. Right let's be off I'm ready for my tea.'

As they gingerly put Seb back in the car Lucy looked across the road and recognised the pub. It was where they had rendezvoused with the Agent, Charles Hopper, when they'd travelled up to have their first look at the Wendover Hotel, as it used to be called. What a lot of water had passed under the bridge since that day – even the Humber Bridge. They were soon home and Garry lifted Seb onto the drive.

'He'll feel a bit sore once the anaesthetic wears off. But don't forget what Mr Wilson said. You've got to find out where that splinter came from.'

'We will. And thank you Mr Ritson. What would we have done without you?'

'That's what friends are for, Lucy. I'll pop round tomorrow to see how he's getting on.'

It had been such an upsetting afternoon with Seb's injury that they all clean forgot about their mother Mandy. No message or text arrived from her to advise them of her train time's arrival. They need not have worried even if they had remembered. Far too engrossed in the Bank Holiday Bingo bonanza, she had clean forgotten to tell them that she was staying on 'a few more days' and would be in touch soon.

32.

It was breakfast time the next morning when Peter spotted the message in the in-box on his mobile from Mandy. It was timed at 00.15 so she must have had a pretty late night. He felt a little guilty at not having kept in touch over the weekend, not that his guilt would have been reciprocated. It simply wasn't. He decided to tell the kids as soon as he read the message.

'Your Mum's decided to stay in Hull for few more days. Maybe her sister's still not too good, although she didn't mention it.' The several seconds of awkward silence were broken by Millie.

'Dad, let's be honest shall we? Mum hasn't settled here like the rest of us has she?'

Peter swallowed hard. It was a tricky moment and one that none of them had publically faced up to yet.

'Sadly, I fear you're right. But let's just jog along as we are for a while. As the Hotel gets busier we can take on some part-time staff to help with the housekeeping. Now, what did the vet say about making sure that whatever found its way into Seb's paw has to be located? Let's get out back and do a thorough search. We'll spread out along the width of the lawn and slowly move towards the end – you know like policemen looking for evidence following a murder. Coats on – it's a bit chilly today.

Make sure Seb stays inside for a while. We don't need him getting the other paw injured. Let's go.'

Twenty minutes later they had reached the far end of the lawn following an almost forensic search.

They had reached the tree that Seb regarded as his own private WC when suddenly Seb, confined to barracks in the conservatory, started barking loudly.

'What's got into him? Hey-up look here, just behind the tree. Look! The hole he seems to be digging to Down Under is about eighteen inches deep. Take a look. There's more soil on the surface than several mole hills added together.'

Peter stepped off the grass, which was overdue it's first mow of the Spring, and peered into the hole which had partially collapsed due the softness of the newly disturbed soil.

'Jamie, be a good lad and get a spade or a trowel or something similar from the shed will you please?'

Two minutes later and Jamie returned with a small spade and a trowel, both covered at the end with hard, dried soil as if they hadn't been cleaned when last used. Peter used the trowel first to clear the loose soil and got quite a shock.

'There's a plank or something down here that looks as if it's been clobbered by a spade and it's struck the wood with some force. It's badly splintered and I'll bet you a pound to a pinch of the proverbial that's where Seb got hurt. Lucy, fetch Seb out but on his lead mind you.'

Before he had even reached the tree Seb started barking again and Lucy had all on to stop him shoving his head down the hole.

'OK take him back in again please Lucy. Jamie, the spade please. I'm going to dig this plank up, if it is a plank that is. We'll soon find out.'

But it wasn't a plank. Fifteen arduous minutes later after taking great care not to further damage the object, the article in question was above ground level on the edge of the lawn. It was the size of a large shoebox and had been perfectly constructed. Although severely discoloured by the surrounding damp soil it somehow retained a timeless dignity all of its own. Lucy spotted something on its surface towards one end, like a brass plate on a coffin.

'Look! Clean it off and see what it says. Go on, Dad.'

Peter used his finger tips to try and rub the grime off but was only partially successful. It was going to take much longer and preferably in the dry and inside. It had just started spitting with rain and they were glad of their coats. He lifted it off the grass to about waist level and gave it a little shake, not violently but enough to ascertain if there was anything inside.

'Get some old newspapers and spread them in good measure on the main kitchen table. Look sharp, it's proper chucking it down now.'

The brass plate was cleaned off with a damp rag to reveal engraved lettering etched quite deeply into the brass. Measuring about three inches square it was fixed to the top of the box by a small brass tack in each corner. The four corners of the box were protected by brass protectors of the sort you see on old suitcases in black and white movies.

The inscription read:

KOALA HOTEL
SCARBOROUGH
1939
NOT TO BE OPENED UNTIL 2039

Jamie was ecstatic.

'Oh wow, it's one of those time capsules. How exciting! Come on, let's open it.'

Peter was more reserved in reaction.

'I don't think we should. Somebody has gone to great lengths to make this box. Look, it's perfect. Those dovetail joints at the corners have been made by artisans. Let's turn it over. Grab the other end Jamie. Gently, that's it. Pass me that rag back.' He started rubbing to reveal a stencilled marking.

MADE BY
DRESSER NELSON
CABINET MAKERS
SCARBOROUGH

'See, this has been specially made for the job. It would be tantamount to heresy to open it. Well wouldn't it?' But Jamie intervened again.

'Dad, I reckon somebody has beaten us to it. Hang on a minute.'

He reappeared holding the clocks and barometer set and held one of its corners alongside the newly acquired treasure trove.

'See! The brass corners are identical. They match the four I found in the shed. Let's gently prise the corners off with a strong knife blade.' Peter reluctantly agreed. One by one they were all gently levered off. They had only been secured with a cheap adhesive and were definitely not part of the original construction.

'See, look! There's a single threaded hole under each one. The screws have been taken out and not replaced – well only by these brass corners anyway. I'm willing to bet that the lid will come off fairly easily. I'll just run the blade gently all round just under the lid. It's a good half-inch thick. What a fantastic box it must have been when it was first made. The heavy lid was soon off and on the table next to the now open box. They all looked aghast and then at each other.

Whatever they were expecting to find, it certainly wasn't this. Peter was quick off the mark.

'Don't touch anything, don't touch anything. I'm going to call North Yorkshire Police on the non-emergency number. Millie, Google it please and make sure it's the local police station and not some goons at County HQ. In fact, halt that. Pop round next door and ask Garry if he can come round as soon as he can. Just tell him we need him please but don't tell him why OK?' Millie jumped to it. She rarely saw her Dad in this mode of action. Garry was there in two shakes of a dog's tail.

'What's up has Seb taken badly?'

'No, but it is Seb's fault. Come and see this.'

'Crikey. Who would have believed it? What a powerful smell. No wonder Seb was going bonkers. I reckon it's cocaine or maybe heroine. Clever the way they stuff it into condoms isn't it? Looks to be about twenty at least. And that looks to be hard cash underneath in plastic bundles. All in Euros by the looks of it – I can't really see without touching. Unbelievable. Don't bother calling the local cop shop. I'll call one of the SOCOs, George Anderson. He's a straight bloke and doubles up as a dog handler when needs must.' He reached for his mobile.

'Hey-up George, it's Garry. Bring your kit and gizmos round to the hotel next to us as soon as you can. Have I got something for you to brighten your day or what?'

'The Wendover you mean?'

'No, its now called the Hotel Scarbados with new owners. How long will you be, roughly?'

'Give me half an hour. Luckily I'm on a day shift today.'

In fact PC Anderson was only twenty minutes and arrived in a blue, yellow and white police van with "Dogs Section" emblazoned on the side. What a good job Seb couldn't read – he'd have had kittens – or even pups.

'So you discovered this in your garden – or rather your dog did?'

'Yes Officer, that's right. Since the day we arrived to look round he's been obsessed with this tree and has been scratching and digging for weeks now,'

'Smart dog eh? Has anybody touched inside the box since you took off the lid?'

'No we were very careful not to. 'We're big fans of CSI Miami and …'

'Thank you young man. I'll take some hi-res photos first of the box and the lid. You can tell its been opened. No screws remaining and jemmy marks all round the edge. I'll need to get some specialist Druds Squad colleagues down here as well. I'm not even going to touch it. Look, one of those condoms has split – hence the smell that attracted your dog. Definitely Class A although I wouldn't pretend to be an expert. I've asked for an urgent response. We don't want your day to be disrupted any longer than necessary. They look like packs of foreign money underneath. I'll just put my latex gloves on and have a careful little feel. Hang on.'

PC Anderson probed gently beneath the money taking care not to contaminate the gloves with any spilt drug.'

There's what looks and feels like a padded envelope underneath only slightly smaller than the dimensions of the box. It's almost as if the box was tailor-made to fit the envelope.'

'Well, Officer, it was definitely a bespoke box. Underneath it gives the name of the cabinet maker.'

'Really, can you remember it.'

'Yes, it's an unusual name – Dresser Nelson. Sounds quite posh doesn't it?'

'Wow. That name rings a bell. If I'm not mistaken their display rooms were just down the road from the nick. But it's years and years ago when I was just a cadet. It'll have cost a pretty penny to make it, even in 1939. Hey-up my colleagues are here already according to the squawk on my walkie-talkie. Can one of you show them in please?'

'Within twenty minutes the box was placed in two separate plastic evidence bags and the narcotics likewise with the exception of the split condom which was packed in one of those transparent airtight envelopes with a sliding seal like peas in a domestic freezer.

The mysterious brown envelope was the last item to be removed from the box. The hand-written words on the front in a semi-copperplate style simply said Hotel Koala, not to be opened until 2039 but it had obviously been opened as the red sealing wax was cracked and broken.

'I think you can keep this. It looks like a letter and a few black and white photos – probably of the original owners. The rest we'll have to take away for forensics. You'll be sent an official receipt in due course. Any questions?' Jamie didn't hesitate.

'Yes, just one, officer?'

'What's that, young man?'

'Can we keep the money?'

33.

They had mutually agreed to save opening the mysterious envelope until after the evening meal. Peter was still somewhat reluctant to proceed but, as Jamie had guessed and the police confirmed, the box had been opened by whoever had secreted the money and the narcotics. The red sealing wax, so beloved by parcel-senders of yesteryear, was definitely cracked but that might have been accidental or just caused by time. Pete's hands were shaking with expectation and he still felt a little guilty. After all, over eighty years had passed since someone, or some people, had gone to great lengths to arrange for the beautiful box to be made followed by the enclosure of the contents and subsequent burial.

'Jamie, you do the honours please. My hands are trembling. I'm still not sure we should …'

The crack in the sealing wax proved only superficial and audibly cracked when Jamie applied a sharp blade between it and the heavy-duty envelope. They were the first people in eight decades to see and read what was therein contained. Jamie passed the envelope to his father.

Peter inverted the envelope so that any contents would slowly slide out onto the table top. In reality it needed more that a little coaxing, so perfect was the fit. At first glance it resembled an old-fashioned legal conveyance in the days that pre-dated Registered Land and Land Certificates. It wasn't paper but ivory-coloured linen card. This was quality commensurate with the craftsman-made box in which it had been contained. It was secured by a green ribbon tied with a perfect bow at the centre. More pangs of guilt hit Peter again as he slowly and deliberately pulled the bow open and as he did so the centreline parted and two equal halves sprung open, left and right, to reveal a manuscript that occupied almost the whole of the centre page. To the left were two photographs, one beneath the other. They were secured by four little triangles of what looked like rice-paper at each corner. Who were they? To the right were two further photographs of much younger people, young adults at first glance. Were they all related?

'Come on Dad, read it out, come on! Who are they?'

'Don't be so impatient. Another few minutes won't matter after eighty years! Now where's my reading glasses. The writing's very fine but written with great care and skill, almost copper-plate. If only folks today could write like this. Do you guys ever use a proper pen any-more? It's all iPads and laptops these days ...'

'For goodness sake, Dad, hurry up. We can't wait. Come on.'

'OK here goes...bear with me.'

I write this short manuscript with a heavy heart. Today we are reluctantly departing our beloved Koala Hotel and there is a possibility that we might never return.

Two weeks ago War was declared against Germany and we have already been notified that the Air Ministry will be requisitioning the Koala. It will be utilised for the convalescence of injured pilots in the months ahead but may it please God that the War will be short and successful.

As a family we came here from Mornington near Melbourne in Australia almost ten years ago. The hotel was newly built when we acquired it and we "Christened" it Koala to remind us of home. Likewise the Eucalyptus sapling we brought with us on the ss Melbourne Star which hopefully has now matured and beneath which we are going to bury the box containing this parchment.

If you have discovered this then we would ask you to respect the grave beneath it of our beloved golden labrador, Duchy,who passed away this summer. She was an Aussie dog and we brought her with us as a puppy. We enclose a photograph of her too standing guard by the front door. She always made such a fuss whenever new guests arrived.

The main photos are of myself Maude Jewitt, my husband Walter and our children Hylda and Bert although we can't describe them as children any more. Bert is an electrician and although a civilian he has been notified that his duties will commence in Plymouth dockyard with the Admiralty within days. Hylda will be working with the NAAFI in York with Army servicemen until further notice.

The box incidentally was made locally from one of the dismantled timber packing cases and other left-over planks were used to make some of the shelving in the dining room. It is solid Tasmanian Oak, a variety of Eucalyptus I understand. It will outlive all of us, I'm sure.

May we wish all future owners of the Koala long, happy lives free of the ravages of War.

Yours very truly,

Maude Jewitt

Proprietress

20th September 1939

There was a long silence followed by little weeps from Lucy as tears trickled down her rosy cheeks.

'Oh, Dad, that is so beautiful. So apart from the drugs, maybe Seb could scent a fellow doggie beneath the tree. I'd like to think so. We must take a photo of him by the front door and mount the two photos together in a nice frame.'

'We will, Lucy, we will. And we must find a special place for this manuscript too. After all it's part of the Hotel's history isn't it? It might be worth telling the local press about our find too. I imagine this wasn't the only Hotel to be requisitioned. On the other hand in view of what else was in the box we might be advised by the police to just hold back until they've made further enquiries.'

A mile away at Scarborough Police Station discussions were already well under way.

34.

PC George Anderson had already handed over the whole case to two colleagues from the Drug Squad who had re-opened the file marked WENDOVER. Systems had of course been totally computerised or digitised for years but surprisingly were still augmented by buff coloured files and folders from time to time. It was reminiscent of the TV series called New Tricks featuring UCOS – an acronym for a Metropolitan Police department Unsolved Crimes and Open-case Squad.

An Inspector from Northallerton and a local Sergeant were now handling the case and in deep discussions over several cups of tea. The Inspector, now the senior case officer, took control of the narrative.

'Well would you Adam and Eve it eh? We thought that was the end of it and then a sodding dog looking for a bone digs this lot up – and a load of brass too. Whose brass is it legally do you reckon?'

'Well, almost certainly the former proprietors' but who knows? Does it legally belong to the new owners now or what?'

'I've no idea. You mean "finders keepers" and all that lark?'

'Does it come under Treasure Trove Rules?'

'Search me, that might be for a Court to decide. Anyway for the moment it's evidence and we must treat it as such.'

'The two sets of fingerprints on the box are liable to be the father, Mr Fishburn, and the son Jamie. But the lab will come back to us later. Forensics will look a lot closer at the wads of banknotes and closer still at the heavy duty polythene they were wrapped in. That will take time. It's not like it used to be when the good old Bank of England could verify the notes and when they were printed and issued. This Euro lark's another ball game altogether isn't it?'

'Anyway we'd best get down to the Wendover and conduct formal interviews with the family. It must have come as quite a shock to them. I said we'd arrive just after two o'clock so we'd best get a wiggle on.'

'Are we going to tell them everything we know?'

'Yes, I think so Sergeant. It's only fair in the circumstances. Agreed.'

'Absolutely.'

Peter and Millie were the only two members of the Fishburn family present when the officers arrived. Jamie was at college and Lucy was out walking with Seb. They took a table in the conservatory overlooking the garden. Ever the hostess, Millie brought in a pot of tea and four cups, The Inspector took charge. Don't they always?

'We will need to take a formal statement from you, Mr Fishburn, just for the file you understand.' He didn't tell him that the file was almost empty and had only been re-opened that morning.

'However first of all it is only fair to appraise you, as the proprietors, of what we know already and..'

'What do you mean what you know already, Inspector?'

''If you'll bear with me please, Mr Fishburn?' He took a sip of tea which being newly poured, almost scalded his lips.

'Your Hotel, previously known for some years as the Wendover, has been under police surveillance for over a year before the Covid outbreak.'

'What! Why? What do you mean under surveillance?'

'You may or may not be aware that along with many seaside towns we have a chronic drugs problem. It's known in the trade as County Lines which unfortunately affords it a degree of legitimacy akin to the centre lanes of certain discount supermarkets. It is anything but, I can assure you. It is highly organised by criminal gangs who send drugs with couriers from bigger cities like Liverpool and Manchester to resorts like Scarborough. But in your case, Mr Fishburn ..'

'What do you mean in my case?! We've only been here five minutes for God's sake and you're calling it my …'

'I do beg your pardon. Let me further explain. I'll rephrase that, in the case of the previous proprietors, who you will recall were called Alvarez …'

'What? Alvarez? Spanish or what? I don't recall that name on the conveyance. In fact I don't recall any name at all. It was all done online during the fag-end of Covid. Those electronic signatures look like spiders don't they? Anyway, sorry for interrupting you. Go on.'

'I am sure that your title to the Hotel is absolute, no doubt about that, but we now have reason to believe that Alvarez might have been an assumed name.'

'Good grief, it gets worse. What next?'

'The Hotel was under surveillance not just for drugs but for suspected people trafficking from Eastern Europe, prostitution and potentially for money laundering as well.'

'I need some more tea. If I was smoker I'd been on my third fag by now.'

'So you see the money in the box is as of equal interest to us as the drugs. We heard within the last hour from the lab that it's Class 1 heroin by the way with a street value of …. wanna have a guess?'

'Twenty grand' chipped in Millie who until now had remained silent.

'No. Double that at least, maybe more. Said Peter. 'We had a case on the Pride of Bruges last year with an Asian crew member getting busted. He didn't realise that crew were treated as a higher risk than passengers. Customs and Excise nabbed him, as we still called it. Estimated value was over a hundred grand.'

'Well I can tell you that the dope in that box beats that by a long chalk. And as for the money, those Euros, at the current rate of exchange, their value is … wanna guess again?'

'No idea, they were too well wrapped up. I couldn't even guess. Go on.'

'Over two hundred thousand Sterling at least. There were five hundred five hundred Euro bills – that's a quarter of a million Euros which equates to about two hundred and ten grand at today's rate. I'll just let that sink in shall I?'

'So whose money is it? Ours? Senor Alvarez or the bloody Exchequer?'

'I honestly don't know, Mr Fishburn, I really don't.' It was the Sergeant's turn.

'One thing's for sure the European staff performing "tricks" for fifty Euros a time didn't earn that sort of money. No, this is big-time laundering – almost certainly from drug dealing and not necessarily from this Hotel. We turned a blind eye to the comparatively minor acts of prostitution. In the grand scheme of things they were just small fry. We needed to catch the big fish. But despite our best efforts, Mr Big never turned up.'

' I knew the going rate was fifty Euros per performance but how do you know, I might ask?' The Sergeant looked more than a little embarrassed.

'This is a tad sensitive so please keep this to yourselves. A junior Detective Constable stayed at the hotel under cover for a long weekend and he, er how shall I say, sampled the goods. Apparently they wouldn't take Sterling and he had to go into Sainsburys the next morning to buy some Euros. He made the mistake of blabbing about in the canteen at the nick and was soon replaced. But then Covid came along and that was that. It marked the end of our investigations – until yesterday anyway. I understand there was an envelope in the box. May I see it please?'

'Of course, can you get it from the drawer please, Millie? It's of historical value only officer.'

'I'll be the judge of that if you don't mind?'

Millie removed all the tea cups from the table before opening the envelope and undoing the bow for only the second time in eighty years. She didn't want some ham-fisted coppers spilling tea and staining it. This was going to be part of the Hotel's history. The Inspector took several photographs of it with his iPhone and seemed satisfied.

'We'll need to take the Hotel Register with us please for the last six months leading up to the Hotel ceasing to trade. The names and addresses of the guests might lead us to make further enquiries elsewhere.

'I'm afraid you can't Officer. There isn't one. We were surprised too but knowing what we know now it's hardly a shock is it? Anybody up to no good would hardly leave a genuine name and address now would they? You don't have to be Inspector Morse to realise that. And when you think about it the last six months trading figures were almost certainly fabricated. Agreed, Inspector?'

The Inspector's ghost was flabbered and he did not appreciate some slip of a college girl trying to make him look silly.'

'And what makes you think that young lady?'

''Because if you're going to sell it then you want to portray as high a turnover as possible, wouldn't you? The last few years accounts might be a total fabrication. Dirty money could have been paid into the bank account purporting to be legitimate takings when all the while the Hotel was a washing machine. Pulling the wool over the eyes of the accountant, not to mention the tax-man, would have been easy. They're not the cleverest people according to my course tutor, Mr White, and if you bother to check with HMRC you'll probably find that they traded just under the VAT limit and …'

'Thank you, Miss Fishburn. I think we'll call it a day for now. We'll report back to you within a few days. Thank you for the tea.'

Back in the police car the Sergeant couldn't help but laugh.

'Ha! Shall I call you Inspector Morse now? Or is it Endeavour? Only joking!'

'One word of this in the canteen and your own forthcoming promotion board will be in doubt – and I'm not joking, Sergeant. Now, back to the station. We've got more work to do.'

Peter was not terribly impressed with his daughter's performance and he told her so.

'Millie, I just couldn't believe how you suddenly started to treat the Inspector like that. You tried to make him look like Dixon of Dock Green. Why?'

'Sorry Dad. But we needed a quick distraction. That Sergeant kept looking down the garden and squinting at the tree like he was itching to go and dig even deeper. You know how sensitive Lucy is and how upset she was about the other doggie. She's already gone and filled the hole in properly and left a little posy of flowers with a heartfelt note. Come on, let's walk down and I'll show you.'

To Duchy
Our Aussie dog from Down Under.
Rest in peace under your special tree.
Lucy xxx

35.

The news from North Yorkshire Police did not sit well on Peter's mind and he did not sleep well to put it mildly. He kept dreaming of the Hotel being full of hookers and drug dealers and he was glad to wake up to find out they were just that – only dreams. Awoken at first light by the first early morning rays of sunshine streaming from the east between the gap in the curtains, he dressed and went downstairs long before the rest of the family or guests. Making a mug of tea he went through the conservatory which resembled a tropical hot-house with the rising sun illuminating those palms and yuccas like never before. Sitting on an ornate bench outside he reflected on the enormity of the events of the last six months, or twelve even, if you allowed for the last six months of Covid infected misery. So much had happened – good, bad and indifferent. The Hotel Scarbados was theirs, the kids were happy but his wife of twenty years had gone. He was realistic enough to think the inevitable – that she might not come back. Pacing slowly round the lawn with steam from his mug still visible in the cool, early morning air, he was brought out of his daydream by the cold nose of Seb whom he hadn't seen follow him outside.

'Hello, Sebbie, me boy. Following me around are you? What do you make of all this eh? If only you could talk, if only you could talk.' Lucy's shrill voice startled him.

'Oh there you are, Dad. I'm going to take Seb down to the sea. Jamie's starting the breakfast routine. Six guests are leaving today and four more due this afternoon.'

'OK. Off you go with Lucy – walkies!'

Peter, Millie and Jamie had breakfast together and mulled over yesterday's meeting with the Police officers. Between them Peter and Millie brought Jamie up to speed as he'd been away at the College at the time. He was thus able to add a viewpoint or two without the affects of actually being present at the time. Perhaps a different perspective would not be a bad thing.

'It's more than a bit spooky isn't it?'

'What is?'

'The fact that this place was under surveillance for a long time. And if I was that Inspector I know what I would do.'

'You do – like what for example?'

'Well look, that was an awful lot of money. Massive. If you had put it there, what would you be thinking of doing in their shoes.'

'You've lost us. What?'

'Well I'd want to come back and dig it up again wouldn't you?'

'Oh my God. We hadn't thought of that. I wonder if the Police have. Maybe the Inspector has already ordered surveillance to recommence. Should we enquire about CCTV and that sort of thing?' Millie was sharp to retort.

'You've been watching too much of Vera and CSI, not to mention Silent Witness.'

'Listen you two. We'll keep Lucy in the dark about this somewhat. She's still young and innocent, not even sixteen yet. By the way I thought maybe a joint celebration between your two birthdays, hers and your eighteenth, might be a good idea. Maybe one day next month? The weather's perked up no end so what about a BBQ in the garden? And if it rains we always have the conservatory as a back up. What d'ya reckon?' Jamie was ultra enthusiastic.

'Great idea, Dad. I'll ask Samantha Lyon for some ideas shall I?'

'Yes by all means but don't forget the vegetarian options or you'll be in trouble. Anyway, I'm popping up to the Cricket Club shortly for my long-awaited chat with that Miles Carter chappie, you know, the Club Treasurer. I'm still intrigued as to what his proposition is. I'll catch up with you two later. And it's time you were off to College, Jamie. Chop chop!'

Peter decided to call Miles first both to confirm the meeting and to get proper directions. He still wasn't totally au-fait with the exact location of the Club despite having been a resident of the Borough for over six months.

'Good morning, Miles. Are we still OK for a chat in your office this morning?'

'Good morning. Sure of course we are. You know how to get here don't you?'

'Er well actually I ..'

'Just head up the hill from the Park. Go past the little cinema on your left and the entrance is second turning on your right. Just drive in the gates are wide open. And don't end up on the wicket – we've just mowed it! See you soon.'

Peter followed the instructions to the letter and on driving through the gates was almost mesmerised by the vista in front of him. He was gob-smacked as they say in Yorkshire. He could see what Carter had meant by not ending up on the pitch which unfolded like a massive green baize snooker table in front of him, albeit fifty yards away beyond rows and rows of spectator seating which dipped in front of him like an ancient amphitheatre. Now where? His phone rang and the blue-tooth kicked in.

'Peter, it's Miles I can see you. I'm on the Pavilion balcony to your right. Can you see me?'

A solitary figure was waving at him from at least a hundred yards away, his other hand clamping his phone to his right ear.

'Turn right and come right down to the Pavilion and park anywhere you like. The only other car is mine. I'll come downstairs now to meet you.' They shook hands.

'Don't tell me you've never been here before, surely?'

'Actually I haven't. Crikey, I never thought it was going to be so huge. How many spectators can you get in here? Two or three thousand I'll bet!'

'At least three times that, Peter, if the weather's good and it's a Yorkshire County match.'

'Yorkshire play here? Here?'

'Well yes, two County games per season at least. We get bigger gates here then they do at Headingley as often as not.'

'I'm amazed. I knew they'd stopped playing at Hull many years ago. I just assumed it was the same with Scarborough. Wait till I tell young Jamie. He was always keen on cricket at school.'

'Did he bat or bowl?'

'A bit of both actually'

'Right let's go upstairs to my office and I'll get Roxie to fix us up some coffee. The start of the season isn't far off but it'll take us a while to catch up on the administration after Covid. What a rum going on it was. Anyway, onwards and upwards and I'll tell you what I've got in mind.'

After a quick five minute tour of the upstairs, the members' Bar and the balcony they were relaxed in Miles's office. Photos of cricketing Yorkshire legends seemed to occupy almost every square inch of wall space.

'Peter, I'll cut to the chase. We're both Yorkshiremen and play with a straight bat, even if you are from Hull – ha ha.'

'Well it used to be in the East Riding as you know until the civil service decided to call it Humberside.'

'You're right there. Listen, if you look at our website you'll see that we're on the lookout for maybe two young overseas players to come and play for us for a four month season.'

'That's not a problem surely. A lovely ground like this should attract plenty of enquiries I would have thought.'

'You've hit the mail on the head – tons of enquiries but it's the personal terms and other financial considerations that prove stumbling blocks. The enquiries all come from either the Southern hemisphere or the West Indies because it's their close season of course. We've had a promising enquiry from a young chap in his early twenties from Bridgetown, Barbados and another from Scarborough Beach in Western Australia. I thought the Barbadian might feel quite at home in the Hotel Scarbados! Which brings me nicely to the question I need to ask you. If any of these youngsters sign up for us for four months can your Hotel provide free accommodation on a sort of sponsorship basis?' This was not what Peter was expecting and he was caught momentarily off-guard.

'Well, er to be honest, I don't know about that. It should be our busiest time of the year. Four months did you say? That'll be May through to September.'

Peter thought quickly on his feet even if he was sitting down.

'I'll need to check with Millie and get back to you. The cost could be considerable to us and let's be honest, Miles, that's not a proposition is it? It's more of a beg.'

'Well the spin-off, excuse the cricketing analogy, could be very useful to you. You'd get a full page free ad in the Festival Programme and I can arrange a nice ad on the boundary hoarding. Have a think about it and call me sometime over the next few days. No hurry. Have you got any questions? I seem to have done all the talking.'

'Just one, Miles. How much is Life Membership for an eighteen year old?'

'Depends. Can he play cricket?'

Like I said, he does a bit of both!'

'More coffee before you go?'

They walked the circumference of the whole ground before Peter got back into his car. His mind was spinning but he needed to talk with Millie first. For the time being they would leave Jamie out of the loop – just in case any deal didn't come off. Twenty minutes later and he and Millie were alone in the kitchen. Their by now customary soup 'n' sandwich lunch was not far away but he needed Millie's attention first. He ran Miles Carter's idea past her. What did she think?

'Dad, I think he's a chancer. You know the old saying – If you don't ask you don't get! If we said, yes OK no problem, I bet you he'd have a big belly laugh. What did Mrs Coates say before they checked out? I'll make sure he treats you right. Remember?'

'Oh yes, clever you, I'd forgotten that.'

'And they also admitted that they're big donors to the Club didn't she? I think there's more to this than meets the eye. I'll bet they've been talking. I doubt they've made any donations for a long time in view of the Cub not functioning for ages during lockdown. Tell you what Dad, let's have a close look at their website shall we? Put the kettle on.' Millie grabbed her laptop and fiddled.

'What is it you're looking for, Millie, this season's fixture list? I don't think it's out yet.'

'It is actually, the first one is a home game against Driffield but that's not what I'm looking for. It's what I'm hoping not to find actually, Dad.'

'You've lost me. Exactly what are you hoping not to find?'

'An advert for any hotel! There aren't any. Good. This is what I'm thinking. We tell Mr Carter that we will agree to provide accommodation for one, just one, overseas player. In return we want a free link on their website to our hotelscarbados.com website for a whole year. Plus the ad on the boundary boards that you mentioned to me.'

'Wow, good thinking. Will he buy that?'

'We'll wait a couple of days then maybe invite him here for a meal, pump him full of Prosecco, and hit him with it.'

Unbeknown to them both two hundred and fifty miles to the south, in a posh office overlooking Berkley Square in Mayfair, a high-flying female executive was sipping her latté coffee whilst playing with her laptop too. She had been planning a trip to Barbados for months and now that travel restrictions were over all she needed was to book a hotel. She Googled 'Barbados hotels' and waited. What came up surprised her:

Did you mean www.hotelscarbados.com

36.

Two days later and Miles Carter arrived for a coffee and a chat, as arranged. The hotel was quiet and any guests with their own cars had long since departed for trips up the coast to Whitby or up onto the moors to see where the much lamented 'Heartbeat' TV series had been filmed. Miles left his modest Mazda in the drive and went to the front door. Before he had even rung the bell Seb trotted out to meet him, wagging his tail as he did so. He remembered his smell from the Opening Night and was probably thinking it was the bloke who drank too much Prosecco. Like Peter had thought a few days earlier, if only he could talk. Millie was on the desk.

'Come in, Mr Carter. Dad won't be a minute. We'll have coffee in the conservatory shall we? Last time it was Prosecco wasn't it if I recall?'

'Er, yes. And rather too much of it if I remember. And as for that gâteau my wife was asking if you could give her the exact recipe and list of ingredients.'

'I'll ask Jamie when he comes back from College later. Let's go through shall we?'

Peter was reading the Yorkshire Post at that moment in the lounge but spotted them almost hidden from view in the glade of palms and yuccas.

'Morning, Miles. I was just reading in the Yorkshire Post about Yorkshire's prospects for the coming season. The sport needs a boost doesn't it after the despair of the last season or two?'

'Good morning, Peter. You can say that again. But you know the rush of folks to the coast after being effectively locked-up for yonks will do us all some good. Now, have you given some thought to my proposition vis a vis providing accommodation for those two overseas players?'

Millie suddenly arrived with a tray bearing three coffees and some chocolate digestive biscuits.

'We have, Mr Carter, and this is the deal as far as we're concerned.

We've done the costings and we are prepared to provide accommodation for only one player – bed, breakfast and evening meal. Laundry is extra, which will be substantial with all those horrid green grass stains on all those cricket whites. This will apply for the months of May, June, July and August only. Over-runs after that period will be charged at the full daily rate and with a 'single occupancy' surcharge at a rate to be agreed. No car parking facilities will be provided but as we are only a fifteen minute brisk walk away that shouldn't be a problem for your young, fit man.'

Carter gulped and spluttered on his coffee. He hadn't expected this. Millie hadn't finished.

'We will have to approve the design of the ad for the Hotel Scarbados which must be positioned immediately in front of the pavilion and as close to the little players' gate and entry onto the pitch as possible. Now, as regards your website, which looks a tad tired to me by the way, we will require a visible link to our own hotel website on the Home page – not one tucked away on page three hidden amongst the Third Eleven's fixtures against Little Morton in the Marsh, if you get my drift. Are we on the same page so far, Mr Carter?'

Carter had visibly paled by now but had little option to go along with it.

'Er, absolutely, yes I don't see any real problems. I will have to get it approved by the Committee of course at the meeting ..'

'Next Monday. But that shouldn't be a problem should it? And finally there is one final condition which will actually cost the Club nothing.'

'Well I'm, er, pleased to hear it.'

So Millie told him of the final condition which was more a polite request really and they all smiled and nodded. Almost on cue Seb arrived at Miles Carter's brown brogues and looked up pleadingly.

'I think he's got his eyes on that last choccy biscuit, Mr Carter. If you want a friend for life you'd best give it to him.'

Seb had barely mopped up the last of the crumbs from the laminate flooring when the front door bell started to ring continuously, as if someone was leaning on it. Peter dashed to the door followed by Seb. He was stunned. At the door was a fifty-something bleach blond with her hair in a smart bob, and expensive looking sunglasses perched atop her head. A skin-tight leopardskin top accentuated the assets that nature had given her and she was dripping in gold costume jewellery. This lady was either a total chav or from Planet Brass. He soon found out she was definitely a native of the latter.

'I say, could someone please remove that awful car blocking your drive? I do so hate Japanese cars. In fact where is your concièrge? Give him my car keys, here. He can park my car for me when the offending article has been moved to the scrapyard. He can also remove my luggage from the boot and take it to my room please. What's my room number? I asked for a room with a view of the Park. I'm assuming you're aware of that?'

'Welcome to the Hotel Scarbados, Miss er and would you like to sign the Register to check in please?'

'Sign in? Sign in? What do think this is? A no-frills airline check-in, darling, at Luton Airport?'

'We always do our best to oblige Miss er …'

'My car's the red Mercedes Kompressor darling Registration PBH 70 in your drive behind that awful ..'

'We'll see to it. The concièrge is indisposed at the moment so I'll get your bags myself. You're in Room 4 on the first floor. Oh and this is Seb who seems to be admiring your boots. I take it they're made from real lizard skin?'

'Do I look like a plastic person, darling? Please show me to my room and do take care with my LV cases -they cost enough I can tell you.'

Peter hadn't got a clue what LV meant but just went along with the flow. This woman was going to be a pain in the neck. He secretly wished that she wasn't staying long – hopefully only a couple of nights at the most. Then he suddenly remembered. She must work for that insurance company that advertises on TV. If only they could afford to do that. Maybe one day they would. With Miles Carter's car out of the drive Peter gently manoeuvred the expensive Mercedes to the car park at the rear God help him if he put so much as a tiny scratch on it. It looked brand new but with those obviously personal plates you just never knew. He removed the lady's two small cases from the boot and took them to Reception but the lady had already gone up to her room. Millie was there.

'Oh there you are, Millie. What a crazy woman. Listen I think she might be some sort of undercover insurance inspector or something. Is our Public Liability Certificate on display as we're legally obliged to?'

'Of course it is. It's up on the wall over there. It's been there since the day we started trading. What makes you think she's an insurance inspector anyway?'

'She mentioned her LV cases. I thought it stood for that huge insurance …'

'Dad, you are a twit, what are you? You have just carried her Louis Vuitton cases inside from her car. That's what she meant by LV!'

Peter felt more than a bit of a chump but laughed it off.

'What is her name anyway? She didn't seem to want to sign the Register.'

'I'll check. Oh well not surprisingly she's got one of those aristocratic signatures where you can only read the first name followed by a curl of the pen that could be in Urdu for all I know. Pamela B. something. Royalty does that don't they, you know like Elizabeth R or George R.? Who the hell does she think she is anyway? All fur coat and no knickers if you ask me.'

'Millie let's be cautious. It's just occurred to me. You don't think she could have been party to the goings on here do you? We need to get her full name. The Police will be back shortly for sure and they will definitely want to keep close tabs on anybody staying here and travelling alone. At least we have her car Registration Number PBH 70 which we also need to put in the Register.'

'Yes, you're right Dad. We don't want that Inspector Morse talking down to us and telling us we're not helping them to help us. Now do we?' The desk internal phone suddenly rang.

'It's room four here. Can I have the dinner menu please? I know I only booked Bed & Breakfast but I've changed my mind.'

'The concièrge, er chef, isn't on duty until six, Madam. I'm not sure what his 'dish of the day' is today to be honest. Can I get him to call you on this number as soon as he's on duty.'

'Please, but not until six. It's been a long and tiring drive from London Heathrow and I'll be taking a rest until then.' She hung up.

'Did you hear that, Dad? London Heathrow.'

'I did but you can't read anything into that, surely. And what's all that 'dish of the day lark' did you just make that up or what?'

'Sort of. Jamie's got a seven day dinner rota – you know, it's Monday so it must be Spag Bol or something, Tuesday it's roast lamb etc. So it's Friday today so what is it today? Fish and chips?'

'I can't remember. Jamie hasn't written it down for me yet.'

'I think we should have the dinner Menu printed on a nice embossed card with a gold border and held on a little easel by the door into the dining room.'

'You mean like this Dad? All I'm waiting for is Jamie's decision. In fact I'll text him on his mobile and ask him to call us as soon as his classes today are finished – about fourish usually.'

In fact it wasn't long before Jamie called in.

'What's up Sis? You need to know today's main course now? Right now?'

Millie explained about the mysterious visitor from London with the expensive car, extravagant luggage and jewellery who would want to eat this evening.'

'Tell her we have a choice this evening of either a lamb Tagine, breast of duck with a Seville orange jus or a vegetarian lasagne with roasted Mediterranean vegetables.'

'Are you winding me up or what? You can't be serious?!'

'You won't believe what we learned today and I'll be a bit later than usual as I'm heading for a butchers in the old Market Hall that Samantha has recommended. It's all ordered and all I have to do is collect it. See ya later!'

Just after six, Jamie called Room 4.

'Good evening, this is Jamie speaking, the Hotel chef. For dinner this evening I'm delighted to offer you ....'

He rattled off the choices that he had told Millie earlier hoping, indeed expecting, the lady to be impressed. He waited seemingly forever for her response.

'The lamb, is it locally sourced or has it spent weeks travelling from the Antipodes in a temperature controlled container?'

For a few seconds Jamie was caught unbalanced but almost instantly recalled the hand-chalked sign in the butchers display less than two hours earlier.

'Actually it's 'New season Texel Wolds lamb. Just in.' Source is Sykes Farms.'

'Excellent, I'll go for that but served with the roasted Mediterranean vegetables please. And none of your mash or chips or other carb stodge that Yorkshire is famous for. I'll choose a dessert later.' She hung up.'

'Dear God, who the heck does she think she is Sis? Anyway it's no problem. We learnt two more dishes today and the tagine was one of them. I'd best get changed and crack on. How many in for dinner tonight?

'Twelve others, all wanting the roast beef and Yorkshires as a separate starter OK?'

Suddenly it dawned on Jamie what 'Room 4' had meant by carb stodge. Oh well each to their own.

Watching her brother preparing the meals in the kitchen it suddenly occurred to Millie that a set of professional chef's knives might make an appropriate gift for his forthcoming eighteenth birthday – top quality mind you. None of your plastic handled stuff from a catalogue. She would do some research, online of course.

37.

The weekend passed comparatively uneventfully apart from 'Madam in Room 4' being as demanding as you could possibly imagine.

'How do I get to Whitby Abbey?'

'Where is Adenfield? I thought they filmed Heartbeat around here?'

'Wasn't The Royal filmed around here too? No, I don't mean the Royle Family!'

'Where is Robin Hood's Bay? Did he really live there?'

She seemed to be short tempered with everyone. Everyone that is except Jamie. On the last night of her stay she asked him to pop into the dining room as she was finishing her flat white coffee with a small glass of Tia Maria. The other guests had retired to the lounge to watch Countryfile on TV and they were alone.

'Thanks for this, Jamie. I want to have a little chat with you in absolute confidence. Do you agree to that and I do mean total confidence?' Not for the first time this strange outsider had caught him off-balance.

'Of course. You have my word. What's up? Something wrong with the food this evening? I hope not. I always try my very best. I'm so sorry.'

'Jamie, relax. Everything's just fine. The orange jus that accompanied the duck could have done with a bit more 'zing' to it but ..'

'I'll make sure next time. Thanks for pointing that out. It wasn't really made with Seville oranges by the way. I've no idea where they came from.'

'Maybe not but description is everything in this game. The more adjectives in the menu the better.

You described the lamb perfectly, it's geographical origin – the Wolds – and even the name of the farm. I was really impressed. Did you make up the name of the farm by the way?'

'No, I didn't. We drove past it many times on our Sunday outings to the coast. It has one of those huge arch signs that you have to drive under – you know like in cowboy films and ranches.'

'Well can I suggest that you get to know the owners of that farm if you can? Wait till you've finished your catering course and then make contact. Ask if you can make a personal visit and go there on your motorbike on a day off. Personal contact is everything. Now before we go any further I think it's time I told you who I am, don't you?'

Jamie just listened for three minutes. Boy, could she talk.

'So now you see why we have to maintain confidentiality.'

You could have bowled Jamie over with a feather.

'Now, tell me a bit more about this course of yours at Scarborough TEC. Who is the senior course tutor or Head of Department? Where's my pen?'

'Her name is Samantha Lyon. When the short course is finished a few of us will be asked if we want to go for the full Diploma. Apparently it takes almost a year but I don't know that I'll be able to find the time off from here. We're only a small family-run hotel and we all have to pull our weight.'

The lady from Room 4 looked him straight in the eye.

'Jamie, I want you to promise me, here and now, that if you're invited you accept the chance to go on the senior course. Go on, promise me!'

'OK, I promise.'

'One more thing. Does the hotel accept Euros?'

'I've no idea. Millie looks after all that side of things. Why?'

'Because I came here more or less straight from Paris where I'd been attending a convention, the first one following Covid. I've got loads of Euros left and I thought it might be a chance to off-load them. Let's treat it as a little test for Millie and see how she handles it.'

She had one more test left for him too but kept that bit to herself.

'I'll be checking out straight after breakfast so I wish you the very best of luck, Jamie. And don't forget – Mum's the word please'.

Madam retired to Room 4. Not for her the Antiques Road Show on TV. She had work to do.

Before eight the following morning, Jamie was on duty in the kitchen dealing with the orders as they came in from the dining room. Little sister Lucy was on shift and came into the kitchen with a scowl on her face.

'You won't believe this. Of all things that dreadful woman in Room 4 has ordered Kedgeree. What the heck is it anyway?'

'No problem, just tell her it'll be an extra ten minutes waiting time and in the meantime give her some more freshly ground Arabica coffee from the sunny uplands of Lower Mesopotamia – and tell me what her reaction is. Can you remember that?'

Two minutes later and she was back in the kitchen.

'Did she say anything?'

'Not a lot but she couldn't stop laughing. I think she fancies you, Bro! Maybe she wants a toy-boy. Mutton dressed as lamb though if you ask me. Mid-fifties I reckon.

Her number plate, PBH 70, is probably her initials and the year of her birth. That makes her fifty-four in my book. Get stuck in there – I bet she's well-minted.'

'And by the way it's not lamb its Wolds leg of lamb basted in Mediterranean rosemary and fresh spring mint.'

'Like I just said, Bro, well minted.'

'Get out of here! It's my kitchen!'

He was starting to sound like Gordon Ramsay. And he hadn't even finished the short 'crash course' yet.

Just after nine o'clock the 'Room 4' lady stood at the reception desk to check out having carried her own Louis Vuitton cases down the stairs herself.

'Good morning, thank you for a lovely stay and may I say what a charming hotel you have. Family-run hotels are always the best – if you can find one that is. Now, I have one last little favour if I may?'

'I'll try to oblige. If you'd like your bags carried to the car my father's not far away.'

'No, no. Would it be in order for me to settle my room bill in Euros please?'

'Alarm bells rang like a fire engine in Millie's head. She knew this blackguard was up to no good. This must be part of the connection and she would call Inspector Morse as soon as the bitch had gone.

'Certainly, we"l give you a fair rate.'

She searched the rate in seconds on her smart phone.

'Shall we call it £1.2 Euros to the pound?'

'That's fine. Let's see so that's three nights plus the evening meals. Were they to your satisfaction Miss Er …'

'Moderate, I would say. Edible but room for improvement. He still has a lot to learn doesn't he? Did you say he's your brother? Mmmm well good luck. Right, I'll say cheerio. Here's my card just in case I've left anything in my room.'

She had deliberately done just that to see how they would deal with it and had put her business card face down on the desk. Minutes later and her flash sporty Mercedes zoomed out of the drive – destination London.

Less than a minute later Millie was speaking direct to "Inspector Morse" at Northallerton and she expressed her reservations, the request to pay in cash in Euros and avoid leaving a trail with a credit card.

'Right, I'll feed that reg number into the PNC. Just a second. Yes, here it is. The registered keeper is a limited company in Mayfair, London. So what's her name, did she leave any ID at all?'

Millie turned over the business card which in her haste she had forgotten about. It was her turn to lose all the blood from her normally rosy and freckly cheeks. It read:

Pamela B. Hesketh BA
Managing Editor
English Hotels Monthly
Email pbh@............

'What does it say on the card, Miss Fishburn? We need to follow it up.'

'Sorry to bother you, Inspector. False alarm. Seems like she's an editor for a posh hotels magazine.'

'Goodness me. Well all I can say is I hope you didn't burn the toast.'

Recovering from the shock Millie now had to break the news to her father, sister and brother. Let's hope that the Kedgeree was up to scratch.

38.

Poor Millie was in a terrible dilemma. Should she tell her father straight away about the true identity of Pamela 'Bloody Hesketh' or not? Maybe that's what the 'B' stood for on her business card, not to mention her personal number plate. In any event Peter was out at the cash and carry with the car. He would be at least an hour and that's assuming he didn't dilly dally and came straight back. No, of course he would come straight back as he had frozen food to consider. She grabbed a coffee and decided to "take five" in the conservatory. It was her little oasis as well as Seb's. He came and nuzzled her thighs as soon as she sat down in one of the colonial-style wicker chairs. She could always rely on Sebbie. Suddenly, her mobile rang in the back pocket of her tailored black trousers. She smiled at the caller ID. It was Katya, her good mate with the website skills.

'Hiya Kat. How are you? Long time no see.'

'Fine ta. Listen, it's just a quickie, hun. Just to let you know I've checked up on the Cricket Club website for you. The link to your hotelscarbados.com website is now live. It works perfectly.'

'That's great, Kat, fab. What can I do for you in return?'

'Well to be honest the Club website could do with a bit of a makeover. It looks more than a bit tired, but after Covid lots of sites are. It needs tarting up, if you know what I mean?'

'Look, tell you what, I'll call Mr Carter the Treasurer to thank him for fixing up the link and at the same time I'll give him your name and mobile number shall I?'

'That would be wonderful. Listen, gotta go hun. Speak soon.'

'Oh before I forget, we'll be having a joint birthday party soon for Lucy's sixteenth and Jamie's eighteenth. You must come for the weekend. Hopefully we'll have a spare room as bokings won't build up that much until the season starts.'

'Great! Text me the date as soon as you know it OK.'

'You bet. Ta'ra, catch you later.'

That was one more box ticked on Millie's 'to do' list. Her father's car was just pulling into the drive. She'd better tell him about 'PBH' before he heard about her from anyone else. Time for some more coffee.

Before Millie could even start a conversation she was beaten to it by her father.

'Hey, Millie, have you seen today's Yorkshire Post yet?'

'What d'ya mean yet? Farming news and sport isn't exactly my scene is it? How long have you known me now for goodness sake?'

'Well, where's our copy? Has it been delivered yet? If that paper-boy gets any slower he'll be delivering yesterday's paper today.'

'Give him a break, Dad. He's only fourteen and it's half-term so he's probably having a lie-in. You know how kids are these days.'

'Rubbish! When I was his age I had a paper round every school day and a pop round on a Saturday and …'

'And you were up before dawn, even in the winter! The paper's in the dining room anyway. What's the fuss?'

'Two chaps were gabbling in the checkout at the cash and carry. Seems like there's a feature in today's Post about Scarborough Cricket Club and the two overseas player's who'll be arriving soon. Apparently it says that accommodation for them is being sponsored by a local Hotel. That's us! I hope they mentioned our Hotel by name. I thought we'd only agreed to paying for one player?'

'That's correct, Dad, But if I've guessed correctly I think our new friends the Coates family are coughing up to sponsor the second player. It doesn't matter to us who pays. But listen, two things, firstly I must tell you my mate Katya called me a short while ago. The link from the Cricket Club website to our own is now 'live' so to speak.'

'Explain, you know I'm not the best at this sort of thing.'

'It means that anyone looking at the Cricket Club website can electronically press a button, so to speak, and up pops our Home Page. Hopefully they'll then take a close look at us and perhaps make a booking. Hotel rooms are still at a premium following the post-Covid stampede to the coast.'

'Well, that's good, Millie, but England's newly rediscovered love of the seaside won't last forever will it? It won't be long before the masses are booking by the million on Wizard Airlines for a fortnight on the Costa Packet, now will it?'

'Dad, we don't know that. It's not just Covid and vaccines and all the misery associated with it that affect people's choice of how to spend their holiday time. Look at all those air traffic controllers in France – they seem to go on strike at the drop of a beret – don't they? And it's difficult to fly anywhere without flying through French airspace – anywhere warm anyway. And who wants to pay good money to go on holiday somewhere that's guaranteed to be colder than where you already are?'

'You've got a point there – several points in fact. By the way has that brassy, sassy horror of a woman in Room 4 checked out yet? Thank God she only stayed here three nights.'

'That's the second point I want to raise with you. Do you know who she was?'

'If I had to guess then I would say an amusement caterer.'

'A what? An amusement caterer for goodness sake?'

'Either she or her husband or family or whatever probably own an amusement arcade in Southend or Clacton or some other down-market slimy resort. Am I right?'

'Er, no, you couldn't be more wrong actually. Here's her business card which she deliberately left on the reception desk seconds before she left. She even carried her own posh bags out to her car. Anyway look, this is her card.' It took several seconds for the truth to sink in.

'Oh my God. What have we done? I hope we haven't upset her? Have we?'

'Not that I know of. But you know what a 'moaning Minnie' she was as soon as she arrived. She never gave up. Her main beef, excuse the pun, was the food. She said Jamie still had a lot to learn. I thought that was bit harsh to be honest. He does his best and his new signature dishes are looking great. She set a little trap by the way when she left.'

'What do you mean a trap?'

'She deliberately left her iPhone charger plugged in by the side of the bed to see if we would find it quickly.'

'Well in her position she's probably got a few spare ones. I wouldn't lose any sleep over that if I were you. She'll leave them all over the country in her job no doubt.'

'No, Dad. I've already sent her a text to tell her we'll be sending it Registered Post to her Mayfair Office today. No doubt you'd prefer it going Sea Mail given your background.'

'Don't be so cheeky.'

'Oh yes, and there's one more clanger I dropped that we can't do anything about.'

'What's that?'

'When she left, before she revealed her true identity, she tried to pay her bill in cash and in Euros.'

'So what? Nothing wrong with that surely. Unusual maybe but hey, brass is brass. On the ferry we took either Sterling or Euros, no problem.'

'But we're not on a sodding ferry are we? In view of her mysterious nature and unwillingness to give her full name, I took fright. I thought she just might have some connection to whoever buried all those Euros under that tree.'

'And?'

'So I phoned that Inspector, you know, the one I called Morse. Within seconds he put her car registration number into the PNC, whatever that is. Anyway that's when he confirmed that the registered keeper is a limited company in Berkley Square in Mayfair.'

'So she's genuine then, at least. In a way that's a relief though isn't it?'

'Oh yes I almost forgot. He says an official letter will come to us soon from Police HQ in Northallerton.'

'What about?'

'No idea. Perhaps he and Mrs Morse want to book in for a long weekend.'

'Enough flippancy for one day, Miss Fishburn. We need friends not adversaries in this game. Just out of interest I'll ask Garry next door what a PNC is. He seems to know everything about police work. Anything else I need to know?'

Three hours later and a red Mercedes Kompressor PBH 70 pulled into Watford Gap Services on the M1 Motorway. She'd drunk too much coffee from the sunny uplands of Mesopotamia before, during and after breakfast and she couldn't hold out much longer. After using the Ladies facilities she powdered her nose and joined a long queue for hot drinks and a snack. The coffee was only luke-warm and the egg and cress sandwich looked as if it had been reared in one of those poly-tunnels that you see on gardening TV shows. No matter. She found a quiet corner seat and looked out at the iron and glass bridge that spanned the motorway and connected the North-bound and South-bound halves of the Services. She pulled her mobile out of her Armani purse and flipped it open. Looks like she'd missed a message earlier, or more likely she hadn't heard the double ping over the noise of her car's sporty engine.

'Hello Pamela. We do hope you enjoyed your stay at the Hotel Scarbados. Your phone-charger is already on its way to your office in Mayfair. The surcharge will be twenty Euros onto your bill on your next visit. Only joking. Safe journey. Best regards. Millie Fishburn.'

Pamela laughed out loud to the consternation of a couple on the next table. She hadn't known that her father had chided her for her inappropriate light-heartedness two hundred miles behind her.

Just for a minute she'd forgotten why she had got out her phone anyway. She had another sip of 'Motorway Coffee' as she called it and pressed the speed dial for her Mayfair office.

'Hi, it's Pamela. Put me through to editorial please. Yes now. Thanks. Hi, it's Pamela. Listen carefully please. I want you to hold the front cover for this month's edition. It hasn't gone yet has it? No, good. I have a new photo for the front cover. Save that hotel in Hastings for next month please. I have one new photo that I took this morning with a hi-res lens for this month's cover. I'll up-load it tomorrow. Is that clear? And did you get the copy I emailed you last night? Good. Yes, it's the centre-spread special. Marvellous. See you tomorrow morning then. Bye.'

She drained the rest of the by now cold coffee and managed to eat one of the triangles of sandwich. Suddenly she had an idea. She carefully peeled off the transparent window from the otherwise cardboard packaging and popped it into her purse. Let's see what young Jamie would make of that. Like his elder sister he obviously had a sense of humour. Did all folks from Hull? Maybe on her next trip she would drive to Scarbados via the Humber Bridge and Kingston upon Hull. Was it really as awful as the 'Hull, Hell & Halifax' jokes portrayed?

Without realising it, she had already made a subconscious decision to pay another visit to the Hotel Scarbados. She would justify it like the 'Hotel Inspector' making a follow-up visit to see if her recommendations had been acted upon.

On the other hand, maybe Lucy's leg-pulling had hit the nail on the head.

39.

Just after lunch the postman arrived with a whole stack of mail. There seemed to be more of it with every day that went past. Apart from the plethora of ads and flyers from pizza parlours, kebab shops and local stores there was trade stuff from kitchen outfitters and furnishers specialising in the hotels and hospitality industry. It was never-ending. It was the task of whoever was on Reception duty at the time to sort the post into two piles – ads and business. Today was slightly different. Two envelopes arrived which fell into neither category. Millie was on the desk and she was pleased that it was her and not her Dad. One was postmarked North Yorkshire and bore the crest of the Police Constabulary. The envelope was addressed to Mr Peter Fishburn. The other was postmarked Humberside and was addressed to simply Peter Fishburn and marked 'Personal.' It was her Mother's distinctive handwriting in blue biro. Oh my goodness. The first letter was expected but quite why the Inspector hadn't mentioned that the letter was already en route, she couldn't imagine. The letter from her Mother, on the other hand, had arrived totally out of the blue.

Millie sensed that both letters were of equal import. She hesitated before taking them through to her father who was still engrossed in the sports pages of the Yorkshire Post.

'Dad, these are both addressed to you. One's from North Yorkshire Police and … well, the other one's from Mum. Here you are.'

To her surprise her father handed the Police envelope back to her. He looked totally dejected.

'Millie, darling, you handle the Police matter for me please. This is going to be difficult for me. Your Mum texted me a couple of days ago. She said it was too upsetting to speak on the phone. She's never been that good on phones anyway has she – unless she's gassing to her sisters? I suspect I know the gist of what's inside. Give me a few minutes will you, love?

'Of course I will, Dad. I'll pop back with some more fresh coffee in a little while. She leant forward and kissed him on his right cheek in as daughterly a way as she could muster. Poor Dad. She could half-guess what was coming too. She went into the kitchen and slit open the official looking communication.

Dear Mr Fishburn

In the matter of our recent investigation I can report as follows.

Our forensic team's results are inconclusive and it would seem that the only prints of quality were that of yourself and your son Jamie. We will thus be happy to return the box itself to you in due course. As you say it has only historic and sentimental value.

The origin of the narcotics is indeterminate although it is highly likely that there was a connection with the high volume of Eastern European female 'workers' at the Wendover Hotel.

This leads me to the large quantity of Euros in the box. The notes were issued on the continent sometime before 2016 by a variety of banks. After that date they ceased to be printed in that high 500 Euro denomination as they were being used for criminal purposes, laundering and other forms of racketeering. They can however be legally exchanged or deposited at your own Bank subject to the usual checks and questions which in this case I suspect will be exhaustive but not impossible.

Finally, I can tell you that as the law stands the money is legally yours. It is being securely held at Scarborough Police Station and we await your further instructions.

Although the case is still technically open, the trail has gone cold and but for the keen nose of your dog the box and it's contents could have remained 'in situ' for many more decades.

Yours sincerely,

Inspector Phillip Mort

Millie read the letter twice to take it all in. Two hundred grand. She couldn't wait to rush through to tell her father. And then she realised that a hundred feet away her dear Dad was probably going through an emotional roller-coaster the like of which he had never been subjected to before. Not to her knowledge anyway.

She looked at her watch, a simple gold quartz timepiece given to her by Mum and Dad on her eighteenth. Those black plastic bracelets that told you your blood pressure and how many steps you'd taken since the last time you'd checked, were not for her. Although quite tech-savvy she was still a traditionalist at heart and she would wear this watch until either it, or her, gave out. Enough time had passed now she thought, and she made a cafetier of coffee.

'You OK, Dad?' She noticed his eyes were a trifle damp. It looked like he'd had a little weepy. Not an Amazon but maybe a little Scalby Beck. She'd recently taken Seb there on "walkies" and was amazed to have spotted a kingfisher and a heron within a few minutes of each other. There was nothing like that in Hull, not within twenty miles anyway.

'Sort of, Millie, sort of. You can read it if you like. In fact I'd like you to, as my eldest.'

'OK but let's pour some coffee first.'

'What kind of coffee is it?'

Millie assumed her best impersonation of her brother.

'It's Fairtrade Arabica from the lower slopes of Kilimanjaro – the first crop of the new season.'

'Ha! OK so it's from the cash & carry, origin unknown.'

'Right first time but I'm sure Jamie can elaborate when he's back from college later. He's doing so well isn't he?'

'He sure is. Here you are, take your time. Even if you didn't recognise her writing you'd guess it's from your Mum.'

Dear Pete

This is the toughest letter of my life and the first two efforts are already in the waste paper bin – you would call it a gash bin no doubt!

The last year has been so tough hasn't it – especially for the kids? When you were made redundant and then Aunt Mary's legacy arrived, we all thought that the move to Scarborough and a fresh start was the answer to all our prayers. Not that I'm particularly religious as you know. I remember you once said that being a mariner you had no option but to believe in God. But now you're a landlubber and I know in my heart that the move is absolutely for the best for our childrens' future. Not that they're young any more of course. They are all growing up so fast and Jamie calls me every few days to tell me how he's getting on. He's taken to it like a duck to water it seems. In another year or so and Lucy will have to decide for herself what she wants to do. Millie sounds as if she could run the Hilton Hotel chain single-handed soon and maybe the Hotel Scarbados will not prove to be a big enough challenge in the longer term. I hope she's not too busy to meet "Mum" and Aunty Gwen for a lunch in Beverley one day soon. You might drop a hint in her direction!

But what about us, Pete? Where do you and I go from here? I think we should tell the kids that we are going to '"legally separate" as they say and that whilst we are not actively seeking a divorce, it is perhaps inevitable in the fullness of time.

Have a think about all of this, Pete. As the late Louis Armstrong sang at the end of the last Bond movie – 'We have all the time in the World.'

Mandy x

After reading it Millie was as damp-eyed as her father. She re-folded it along the original crease lines and replaced it in the envelope which bore a new first class stamp with one of those dreadful URL codes attached to the side.

'Here, keep this safe, Dad. In the years ahead you might just want to look at it and remember.'

The letter from North Yorkshire Police was still on the coffee tray. What a dilemma. It was hardly the appropriate moment to tell him that they were all two hundred grand richer. Now was it? On the other hand it wasn't right to keep the news from him. She decided on a compromise and would share the news with all the family after dinner that evening. Her mobile pinged. It was Katya.

'Hey Millie. Have you checked your website? It's had just under a thousand hits in the last four hours. Can you believe that?'

40.

Dinner was over and the resident guests were either in the lounge making friends with strangers or had gone to their own rooms. Not all of them wanted to watch the re-run of Fawlty Towers. What a good job that Hotel Scarbados wasn't managed along the same dysfunctional lines. It was almost boring by comparison but that's what most folks had come for – a bit of peace and quiet.

'Jamie that roast beef was just perfect tonight. What cut was it?'

'Didn't you read the menu, Dad?

More out of curiosity Pete picked up a spare menu and donned his reading glasses.

Potage du Jour
Slow-roast brisket of Vale of York Aberdeen Angus
Pomme de terre rosti Mange tout Cauliflower au gratin
Profiterole au crème freche Gâteaux de la maison
Cafe Columbia ou Java

Peter didn't know what to say but before he could even begin formulate a response Millie interrupted proceedings.

'Listen up everybody, this is important.'

She had practised what she was about to say several times as she wanted to get the tone just right. She had the envelope with her and flashed the front of it with the North Yorkshire Police motif on the front so that they could all see it.

'This is the initial report and conclusion from the Inspector in charge of the investigation into that box and its contents. I'll read it out to you all in full.'

Dear Mr Fishburn ....She read the first few paragraphs out and then paused.

'That's all very interesting but it's the penultimate paragraph that really counts. Listen carefully.'

'Finally, I can tell you that the money is legally yours. It is being securely held at Scarborough Police Station and we await your further instructions.'

The silence was deafening but was eventually broken by Peter who was also clutching another envelope with a very different content. He stuttered and hesitated but in his heart he knew he had a duty to perform.

'I am sorry to have to contrast that amazing news with some that is very personal but which will affect all of us deeply, possibly for the rest of our lives.' His eyes were already dampening and he wondered if he would be able to control his emotions. Sensing his distress, Millie went to sit so close to him you could not have put the proverbial cigarette paper between them.

'Millie read this letter this morning when Jamie was at college and Lucy was out walking Seb.'

At the mere mention of his name Seb momentarily looked up from his doggie-bowl where was slowly devouring the portion of beef that Lucy had swapped for extra cauliflower cheese.

'I have thought very carefully about doing this but I have decided to read this letter from your Mum to you in its entirety.

*'Dear Pete .... This is the toughest letter of my life
.... We have all the time in the world.'*

Only Lucy showed any immediate emotion and she immediately rushed over to her Dad and threw her arms around his neck. The line in the letter where her Mum had said that she 'would have to decide for herself what she wanted to do' had cracked her up. She already knew what she wanted to do and she had a bit of news to give them but this really wasn't either the time nor the place. It could wait a day or two. But she had made up her mind and those stubborn Viking genes she had inherited from her mother were stuck to her double-helix like super-glue.

'Let's make some coffee, Jamie.'

'OK, you've seen the menu. Java or Columbian? And when Mum said I had taken to my new profession like a duck to water, did she mean an Aylesbury duck from the cash and carry or a hand reared Gressingham duck basted in honey with a jus of Seville ...?'

Peter smiled for the first time that day. With just a few words his only son had removed all the tension from the meeting. Paradoxically, the vast sum of money had almost been forgotten. His family was far more important to him than anything else. No doubt Millie would be consulting her financial guru, Clive White, about exactly what to do with it.

The clanking of Seb's bowl snapped him out of his thoughts. He had snaffled up all the remaining brisket and rich gravy. Had he been able to speak he would have told them that, in future, he would prefer all his meat 'on the bone.' Don't humans ever learn? And what was all the fuss about that flippin box?

They all watched the tail-end of Fawlty Towers and went to bed with their own thoughts. Tomorrow was another day which would bring more news and challenges. Millie checked the hotel's email in-box before turning in. With all the upset and developments of the day she had clean forgotten to perform this simple and routine duty. She did a double-take. There were more than twenty requests for room reservations. They would have to wait until the morning.

41.

Straight after breakfast Millie started to tackle the long list of enquiries which seemed to come from all parts of Yorkshire although with email addresses you never could tell – unless the sender added something personal like 'We come from Barnsley every year to watch some cricket' or 'Let's hope it's warmer than Ilkley – with or without an 'at?'

She reached into the drawer for the rudimentary room-planner cum calendar that she had designed herself. The spin-off from the Yorkshire Post story had produced immediate benefits and the link to their own website was already working a treat. That reminded her – there was still no word on the precise arrival dates of the two young cricketers from Barbados and Australia. She had blocked off two garden-facing rooms for almost four months but the month of May and the start of the season for the First Eleven had already started. It was looking like lost revenue – like a plane that had taken off. Once airborne you couldn't put a fare-paying bum on the seat, as the travel jargon had it. Her home-made manual booking system was already taking the strain. They couldn't justify the use or the cost of a full-blown computerised booking system. They weren't big enough. And if only she had a little office off the hall. The reception desk and it's drawers were already starting to bulge. She was about to phone Mr Carter at the Cricket Club to enquire about the overseas players when out of the blue the phone rang and it was the man himself.

'Good morning, Millie. It's Miles Carter at the Cricket Club.'

'Good morning to you too, I was just about to call you actually – you've saved me the trouble.'

'Well actually, I'm calling in connection with the two chaps coming from …'

'Oh that's great. Their allocated rooms are empty and if we could I'll let them be used right up until their arrival. Otherwise it's just wasted revenue.'

'Ah, well I'm afraid to say it's not good news. Quite the opposite actually. I don't quite know how to tell you this. Unbelievably, we've received two emails over night. The first one's from Australia which is nine hours ahead of us so it was probably in my in-box before I'd even gone to bed. I'll read it to you shall I?'

'Please do.'

Dear Mr Carter

I regret to tell you that my current Club, Western Warriors C.C, are insisting that I honour my existing contract which doesn't expire for another two months. Following the lifting of all Covid restrictions here in WA, the season's fixtures have have had to be re-jigged in order not to lose money. I am not therefore available to come to Yorkshire until mid-July. In the circumstances I am thus requesting that our arrangement is put 'on ice' for a year. As we say here in Western Australia – we'll have to do a WA which over here stands for Wait Awhile. Perhaps you could give me your thoughts in due course. Yours etc.

'Millie, it get's even worse, I'm afraid. I've just taken a call from the young Barbadian chap in Bridgetown, Barbados. It's seven o'clock in the morning there. He was so upset.'

She glanced up at the twin clocks on the wall. Yes, that's right, four hours behind.

'You're not going to believe this. Apparently, Barbados has just changed its Constitution and is no longer a constitutional monarchy with our King as Head of State. The knock-on affect is that whilst a work permit to play here will not be denied, the associated paperwork to make it happen will take many more weeks. It's awful. I thought I'd let you know as soon as we found out.'

Before Miles Carter had even finished speaking Millie had taken her red pen to the room planner. It was time to start filling in the gaps in the 'vacant rooms' squares. Bye-bye Barbados, hello Barnsley. Bye-bye Perth, hello Pontefract. It was like playing that game 'Battleships' and the number of squares to fill in was decreasing with every day that went by. She was just about to make herself a coffee when the postman poked his nose into Reception.

'More post for you guys. You're getting busy aren't you? Crikey, it was never like this with the Wendover.'

Millie sorted the incoming post into the usual two piles but once again an envelope didn't fit into either category. This was a plain white one, hand written and addressed to Jamie Fishburn. The post mark was Mount Pleasant London, one of the capital's major sorting offices. A first-class stamp had been manually fixed. There was no other clue as to its origin. And then, right at the bottom of the pile beneath yet another Pizza ad, was another white envelope, this time a window envelope addessed to Miss Lucy Fishburn. It was franked and the mark gave the sender's name as Andrews Veterinary Surgery. 'Ah, thought Millie, that'll be the vet's invoice for the emergency treatment to Seb's paw all those weeks ago. But why wait all this time? And why send the bill to a still under-age girl who couldn't write out a cheque even if she was on the bank mandate. It was all very odd but she put it onto the kitchen table where Lucy would no doubt spot it later when she came back from "walkies" with Seb who had now fully recovered from his accidental brush with a quarter of a million Euros. Jamie's envelope went onto the same table. He would be back from college and now that an account and deliveries had been arranged with the butcher he didn't have to divert there on his way back. He'd hand written out today's menu for his sister to print on the menu template. That was her next task and she read it through quickly before printing it out.

Tomato and basil soup OR Cullen skink
Pork fillet cordon-bleu OR Cod meunière
Asparagus tips Jerusalem artichokes Petits-pois
Dauphin potatoes Early Nantes carrots au buerre

It was starting to get to Millie, this posh nosh. But Jamie was full of it and who was she to knock it? Cooking wasn't really her scene but hey, with a Master Chef wannabee in the family, why should she feel guilty. Mum had always spoilt them with her own homely but adequate culinary skills and her little Bro. was doing the same That reminded her to give Mum a call later. She had sourced an online supplier of French-made chef's knives and thought it might be a good suggestion as a present to Jamie from her. On no account did she want her Mum to feel out of it. No way.

Millie completed the room reservations requested by the plethora of emails. Mr White had advised her that a fifty percent occupancy rate would more than cover there overheads, including modest drawings for all of them. Currently running at between sixty and seventy percent there were no worries on that score.

Peter came back from the cash and carry which was becoming an almost daily routine now. After unloading the frozen and other food into the freezers and fridges he noticed the two white envelopes on the kitchen table. He peered at both of them.

'Hello, what's that? I wondered when we were going to get a bill. They can't be short of brass can they? And who does Jamie know in London.'

'Dad, I've no idea. Here's Lucy now.'

'Letter for you, Lucy. It's on the table.'

'Thanks, Sis. Been expecting it.'

'Dad says is it a bill for Seb's treatment?'

'No, it isn't. We won't be getting a bill anyway. I'll explain after supper tonight. Is Jamie back from college yet? '

'No why, did you want him?'

'Yes, I've seen tonight's menu and I don't like it. Seb prefers beef to pork. He knows that.'

Jamie wasn't long in returning from his course and had plenty of time to prepare the evening dinner.

'Heck, a letter for me? From London? I don't know anybody in London – in fact I haven't been there since Mum and Dad took us on that trip to Regents Park Zoo. And that's a few years ago now. Pass me that knife will you please?'

'What is it? Who's it from?'

'You won't believe this. It's a wrapper from a sandwich pack – you know those plastic triangle things. There's a note inside from Pamela Hesketh. It says 'please re-describe this label and post it back to me. Is she having a laugh or what?'

42.

After dinner the four of them had the now almost customary chat over coffees around the large kitchen table. In many ways it was their own little oasis from the hotel and the guests but they were always 'on call' as it were for any requests from guests for a beer or a glass of wine to accompany the now expanding repertoire of Jamie's menus. Soon Jamie would be eighteen and if time allowed from his chef's duties, would be able to help his father out with Bar duties. Knowledge of wines was not covered in his 'crash course' but it would be a whole module should he be selected to study for the full Diploma starting at the end of the main holiday season in September. Just what did he have to do to impress the Head of Department, Samantha Lyon?

'Jamie, it's high time we set a date for your and Lucy's joint birthday party.' Peter reached for a calendar and started ticking off certain dates.

'So, you two, how do you want to play it?' Lucy was quick off the mark.

'I think a Bar-B-Q on a Sunday lunchtime going into the afternoon would be ideal.'

'Wouldn't a Saturday be better, Lucy?' said Millie.

'No! Definitely not. No!'

'They had never seen her so adamant. Did it really matter that much?'

'OK, I might as well tell you something now. I was going to wait a while but in the circumstances I guess it's better now.' She reached into the back pocket of her blue jeans and pulled out the folded envelope from the vet that had arrived in the post that morning.

'Its from that nice Mr Andrews, the vet who treated Seb shortly after we arrived. Shall I read it to you, it's not long?'

Everyone was mystified. Despite the mention of his name, Seb carried on chompimg on his pork cordon bleu but he must tell them 'steady on the cheese next time and what happened to the beef.'

Dear Lucy

I am writing to offer you a period of "work experience" in our Practice commencing in two weeks time.

Initially this will mean eight hours a week, four hours on a Saturday and another weekday of your choice. You will not receive payment but we can offer you a generous transport allowance in part compensation. It will stand you in good stead if you one day decide to become a qualified Veterinary Nurse. Your passion for animal care is obvious from the way you assisted me all those months ago.

Should you decide to accept I would be happy to give you details of how this might eventually lead to a Diploma in Veterinary Nursing.

I look forward to hearing from you by letter, email or even a phone call.

Yours sincerely,

Andrew Wilson BVMS

Pete's reaction was immediate and straight from the heart.

'Oh, Lucy, how wonderful for you. Come here, love.'

The kiss and bear hug would have done a six foot grizzly proud. Jamie went straight to the fridge and opened a bottle of Prosecco.

'This is from the '21 vintage and rolls off the palate with hints of minerality, almonds and …'

'Shut up Jamie, give it a rest and get pouring.' was Millie's reaction. She immediately thought back to a line in the heartfelt letter from her mother to her father which she had read out loud only twenty-four hours earlier:

'In another year or so Lucy will have to decide for herself what she wants to do.'

How prophetic her Mum had been. What else would come true? She kept those thoughts to herself.

The date for the joint Birthday Bar-B-Q was set for two weeks hence on the Sunday, so as not to clash with Lucy's work experience. Millie drew up a rudimentary guest list which included her Mother and Aunty Gwen. So did Jamie, but his list also included a certain lady in Mayfair.

43.

The next morning, after breakfast during the lull, Millie put in a call to Clive White – her adviser and effective de facto bank manager, even if he was retired. It was a long call, much longer than she had envisaged. She had an awful lot on her mind.

'Hi Mr White, er, Clive. Yes all is well here thank you. Maybe even too well.'

'Millie, how can that be? Too well?'

She went on to explain that the new website with its catchy name had caught people's imagination and that the spin-off from folks Googling Barbados Hotels had resulted in more than a few enquiries already. That included Pamela Hesketh and how she had already paid them a visit, albeit undercover until the exact moment of her departure.

'Crikey not the Pamela Hesketh surely? The English Hotel's Monthly editor? You're kidding me. Pull the other one!'

'No I'm not joking. She stayed here three nights and moaned almost continuously about this, that and the other. A nightmare she was – until she checked out and then she seemed to morph into quite a pleasant lady. Quite charming in fact. She complained how awful the food was to me but in secret was apparently complimentary to Jamie. In fact she wrote to him only a couple of days ago.'

'Oh my God, you have no idea how influential she is in the business. She can make or break you. When I was still a

Branch manager in Hull she paid an undercover visit to one of the motels on our books, in Cleethorpes if I remember. Anyway the review she put in a subsequent issue of her magazine was almost defamatory. It was only two or three column inches but every negative detail was magnified threefold – Grubby towels, burnt toast, dim lightbulbs. You name it. She even mentioned that the phone charger which she had accidentally left in her room was not returned to her. Can you believe that? She even moaned about an unfriendly dog, a German Shepherd, that had tried to take a chunk out of her ankle and her Armani purse.'

Millie froze. Thank God she had posted back that iPhone charger the next day.

'Anyway, the bottom line was that her review destroyed the business. To be honest the proprietors weren't the sharpest tools in the box. They took no notice of the advice I gave them at their annual review at the Bank. No notice at all. They just blundered on in their own sweet way. The last I heard the hotel was on the market. Finito!'

'Well thanks to you and others we now have a problem of a different nature.'

'What's that?'

'We're full! Until the middle of September anyway. Just rammed. The link and connection to the Cricket Club has seen to that. And those two overseas players both can't come at all now, not this season anyway. So those slots have been filled up.'

'You could maybe try one of those online booking agencies that seem to pervade these days, Millie.'

'No, definitely not, Clive. Just a few days ago I was listening to Georgey, my favourite presenter on BBC Radio York. She was interviewing a B & B landlady not far from here who was waiting for thousands of pounds from one of those agencies for weeks. They got the money in the end but not after a lot of hassle and too many sleepless nights. No, we'll do it our way, Clive. Oh yes I almost forgot tell you. How could I possibly forget? Remember that bundle of Euros that Seb sniffed out? Well we've confirmation from the Police that legally it's ours. Over two hundred grand in Sterling. We still haven't got our heads around it, to be honest.'

At the other end of the line, Clive gave out a long, low whistle, almost as good as the opening bars of The Good the Bad and the Ugly.

'Wow, wow, wow. And you almost forgot to tell me, for goodness sake?'

'Well we have had rather a lot on.'

He just couldn't believe how Millie had matured, business-wise, in such a short time. Talk about an old head on young shoulders.

'There is another solution you just might like consider which we can talk about at length when we next meet …'

'Oh, that reminds me, Clive. We're holding a Bar B Q here at the Hotel for Jamie's eighteenth and Lucy's sixteenth. It's two weeks this coming Sunday. You and Mrs White are invited of course. Sadly we don't have any vacant rooms left to offer you an overnight stay.'

'That's fine either she or I will drive and not drink. It's only an hour in the car, traffic permitting. It can't be as bad as last time when it was like cattle being allowed outside of the fold-yard for the first time after winter. Can it?'

Millie wasn't a big fan of 'Countryfile' so she wasn't too sure about his analogy. After they finished the call Millie wondered what he had meant by 'another solution.' No matter, it could wait.

Meanwhile, down in Mayfair, the most expensive property on the Monopoly board, Madam Hesketh was laughing so loudly she could be heard all over the open-plan office. She had just opened the envelope and enclosures from Jamie in Scarborough.

Hi Pamela

OK how about this:

This egg and cress sandwich is no ordinary egg and cress sandwich

The free-range eggs are perfectly married to the lightest fat-free mayonnaise

With just a suspicion of Mediterranean Cayenne pepper to stir your imagination

The granary bread is from Norfolk's golden wheatfields

The watercress isn't grown on a kitchen window box but comes from locally harvested

chalk streams as clear as gin …

That's the best I can give it. Don't forget my 'Coming of Age Party' two weeks on Sunday. Looking forward to seeing you again.

Jamie

Pamela reached for her diary. She wasn't going to miss the opportunity to see him again. Perhaps she would go by train this time, after all it was a long way and Kings Cross and the LNER to York was only a few stops on the Tube. She booked return tickets online and electronically stored them in the wallet of her iPhone. Now, I've only got two hours to finish that review she thought. She had all the information and copy that she needed. No time to lose!

Thirty minutes after Clive White had spoken on the phone with Millie he called her back. He couldn't possibly wait another two weeks. Not with the extra news she had imparted to him.

'Hi Clive, did you forget something?'

'Millie, you weren't even born when it came out but you know the film "Jaws" about a killer shark that terrorised a New England resort?'

'Sure, we've got the DVD somewhere. Why?'

'Remember that bit where the guy with the fishing boat who was trying to catch it said 'We're gonna need a bigger boat.'

'Yeah sure, why? It's a famous line. So what's up?'

'The same applies to you, Millie. You're gonna need a bigger hotel.'

44.

Clive White's last words of 'You're gonna need a bigger hotel' rang in Millie's head all day, like an ear-worm of words instead of music. Did they really need a bigger hotel? They were so settled, despite all the trials and tribulations of the last year. Jamie was about to finish his crash-course in catering with high hopes of being accepted for the full Diploma course, Lucy looked as if she was about to pursue another avenue in a field she absolutely loved. The hotel was fully booked until the end of September and even beyond then bookings were arriving every day. It was almost too good to be true. The mere thought of starting all over again was brain-numbing. Even if they could sell the Hotel Scarbados quickly, where would they go? How big a hotel? How many rooms? Where exactly? Maybe she, her father and Clive should meet and have an in-depth talk. Perhaps Clive and his wife could come an hour or so earlier before the big birthday party got under-way. Needless to say Jamie was organising the catering and Samantha Lyon had insisted on becoming involved. She had a surprise for him following a phone call and a suggestion from Pamela Hesketh. She had chided Jamie when he told her that Pamela was invited. Too late now. Millie had no idea that within the hour the postman would deliver a large white envelope that would change their lives once again. So would the smaller white one but not just yet.

'Postie! I've left it on the desk top.'

'Thank you!'

What was it this time? The usual ads and flyers with a couple more that looked a bit up-market including one for the Stephen Joseph Theatre in the Round. She glanced briefly at it and noticed that a play based on Klimt's painting '"The Kiss"' was showing for two nights – on Jamie's birthday and the night before. She wouldn't mind seeing it but the hotel would be packed and preparations for the Bar B Q all-consuming. She moved on to the large white envelope and slit it open with a newly acquired silver paper-knife. It looked so much more civilised than a kitchen knife. A glossy magazine slid out, front cover down, onto the desk top. It looked like an aerial view of a country manor in the Cotswolds and was obviously taken by a drone. Either that or a high-altitude sparrow. It looked like the sort of place that started at two hundred guineas a night – without breakfast. And I bet they don't even serve kedgeree thought Millie quietly to herself. Who could afford those sort of prices in this day and age? She casually flipped the magazine over to the front cover. She nearly had a whole litter of kittens.

Millie simply couldn't believe what she saw in front of her eyes. Occupying the whole of the front cover, which bled to the very edge, was a colourful photo of the Hotel Scarbados seemingly set in a glade of palm trees. Sitting right in the drive was Seb, looking every bit the owner not the guard-dog. Apart from the title of the magazine 'English Hotels Monthly' and the month of issue and the bar-code, all it said on the front cover was – Hotel Scarbados – this month's centre feature.

It took time to sink in but eventually she plucked up courage and with some trepidation unfolded the publication to the centre pages. She was totally bowled over to see a mélange of no less than eight other pictures showing the reception area with the clocks and barometer over the desk, dining room, the conservatory with its new brass fans and of course more palms accompanied by the yuccas with what looked like a Caribbean sunset projected to the walls. It was simply mesmeric and at first she could barely recognise their own hotel. The short but lucid Editorial was even more flattering. She read it quietly to herself several times:

'Tired of flight delays, jet lag and mosquito bites? Then do what I did and go to 'Scarbados' on the Yorkshire Coast and stay at this wonderful family-run hotel. The Fishburns have only owned and managed this establishment for six months but already their own in-house chef, son Jamie, is making his marque in the culinary world. Don't take my word for it. Book in for a long weekend and see for yourself. Even the egg sandwiches for my packed lunch were the work of a future star. Watch out, Jamie Oliver. James the Second isn't far behind you. Will I be going again? You bet. I've cancelled Barbados and booked again for Scarbados! Ed.'

For the second time in a few days Millie cast her mind back to the auspicious words in her Mother's heartfelt letter to her Father – 'Jamie's taken to it like a duck to water.'

In her excitement Millie almost forgot to open the second envelope. Its contents were almost as extraordinary and unexpected as the first envelope. It was a single sheet of high quality vellum paper, a hundred and twenty gram parchment at least. Who on earth was this from? She unfolded it carefully and a brightly coloured, embossed coat of arms in the top right-hand corner immediately caught her eye. It was the official insignia of the Republic of Barbados depicting a fish and a pelican either side of a shield-mounted tree. The motto Pride and Industry was embossed beneath. The letter was short but friendly.

Dear Sirs

My wife and I are disappointed to learn that our nephew, Courtney, will not be playing for Scarborough Cricket Club in the foreseeable future. Despite trying to pull a few strings, as they say, the delay makes it more practical for him to wait until next year.

Courtney had told us how much he was looking forward to seeing you and staying at the Hotel Scarbados. We were hoping to pay him a visit for a few days to watch him play and join him at the hotel. If you have any vacancies in mid-September then perhaps we could still do that? It would be nice to send Courtney a first-hand report, so to speak.

Perhaps you would be kind enough to let me know, preferably by email.

Thanking you in anticipation.

Yours faithfully,

Malcolm Morgan
High Commissioner to the United Kingdom

This was almost too much for Millie to take in for one day. She didn't really believe in astrology but she thought it might be a good idea to check her Stars in the paper later. She thought she'd better tell her Dad about the day's events and it was still only lunchtime. Where would she start? The 'bigger boat', Barbados or the the magazine? Where was her Dad anyway? Yet again he'd been at the Cash & Carry. If only they delivered but the very name gave away how they operated. Eventually he returned and unloaded the car's contents.

'You know what, Millie? We're going to need a bigger car soon – or a van or something. Any more than this and I'm going to have to make two trips in future. Make us some coffee, I'm knacked.'

'Dad, I need to run a few things past you. Let's go into the conservatory. You carry the coffees. I just need to collect a couple of things from reception first.'

Millie showed him the magazine first, then the letter from the Barbados High Commissioner. He was careful not to spill the coffee in shock over either of them. Mentally he was already framing that letter with its colourful Coat of Arms.

'It won't half look good on display alongside the clock on Barbados time won't it. You know in the hotel reception.'

'Maybe, but which hotel?'

'What do you mean which hotel? This one of course.'

'Dad, Clive White and I had a lengthy conversation this morning'

'Nice guy, so what did he say?'

'Dad, do you remember that film Jaws ….?'

45.

Clive White's opinion that they would be well advised to start thinking about the possibilities of an up-grade to a bigger hotel, floored Peter. Where would the extra money come from, a Christmas cracker? Yes, the hotel generated small profits but not the tens of thousands needed to buy a bigger place. And who in their right minds would buy the Hotel Scarbados, about which gossipers had already started gibbering about its past history, call girls and the like. Maybe somebody at the police station had tipped the wink to a local journalist in exchange for a free lunch. They'd had more than a few odd calls recently along the lines of: 'Good evening, is Natalia available tonight. I had her last time?' Another asked for 'two lines of coke, mate, and I don't mean Diet Coke.' There was gaiety and sniggering in the background and the number was 'withheld' so it was probably a call from a pub. To be honest he was getting tired of it. Maybe, just maybe, Clive's idea was sound and should be pursued. Deep down he was also aware that, morally at least, his wife Mandy deserved the lion's share of that cache of Euros. They hadn't even told her yet. He would mull on it pending the pre-party talk with Clive on Sunday.

The rest of the week simply flew by and suddenly it was Saturday. All the meat had been delivered by the butcher for the BAR B Q the next day and the kitchen started to resemble a giant food hall as Jamie prepared the various marinades for the beef, pork and lamb in various cuts and styles.

'Butterfly cut' fillet steaks received special attention and would be proffered towards the most important attendees. Fortunately Lucy was out at her first day of work experience at the Veterinary Surgeon's as the sight of so much meat on display would have upset her beyond measure.

In late afternoon a white Station Taxi pulled into the drive and the rear passenger door opened. The driver pressed the boot-release lever and the lid slowly climbed skyward. A smartly dressed lady swung her long booted legs in parallel to reveal a cream coloured dress with a black and gold belt around her narrow midriff. The Armani purse was unmistakable. It was Pamela Hesketh on her return to Scarbados. The driver carried the now familiar LV bags to the front door of the hotel as Seb sniffed approvingly around the Chanel No. 5 mist that followed her every step.

'Hello darlings. Soo good to be back. Am I in the same room as before? Room 4 wasn't it? Where I accidentally left my phone charger. Ha ha! I think I'd better sign the register properly this time – oh I see you've got one!'

Millie did the honours just as she had done before but this time the atmosphere was totally different.

'And where's our young celebrity chef? Ah, here he is.'

She gave him two air kisses, left and right mwa, mwa! He was a tad embarrassed, unused as he was to flash southern women paying him close attention but he was genuinely flattered. The party wasn't until the following day, almost twenty four hours hence and he did wonder how they were all going to entertain her. They needn't have worried but they weren't to find out until straight after dinner. It was a warm evening and even after dinner the sun was still shining although the early hints of autumn were just beginning to show. The distant lights of the Tree Walk in Peasholm Park were glinting through the oak and sycamore trees a few hundred yards away and visitors were still promenading around the edge of the man-made lake created over a century earlier. What foresight the Edwardian landscapers and tree planters had possessed to project beauty and pleasure for generations to come. Scarborians, or is Scarbadians, were so lucky to live in this little jewel by the sea.

Pamela had changed straight after dinner into a long black pencil shirt with a tight cream blouse with matching jacket and evening bag that was just about big enough for a Chanel refill, some lippy and a small hairbrush. Where on earth was she going in this part of town in that garb? She hovered in reception with a half-drunk Margarita until she saw him coming down the stairs wearing a flash navy blazer with buttons, pips and epaulettes seemingly all over. His smile was as wide as Peasholm Glen.

'Ah, Peter, there you are, Honey. The taxi's outside. I've been dying to see Klimt's "The Kiss" since it was released. So glad you could come with me, babes.'

Lucy was wrong. Jamie was the sprat, not the mackerel.

46.

The next day, Sunday, brought glorious late September weather. Many a Scarborough resident will tell you that the resort gets some of its nicest weather in this month and that's without the effects of global warming, climate change or El-Niňo!

With breakfast over and most of the guests out for a walk in the Park or along the seafront to Scalby Mills, it was time for the family to snap into action for the big party. There was so much to do. Extra garden furniture was taken out onto the rear lawn and umbrella's stored. The forecast was 'dry and clear' with not even a Michael Fish type hurricane within a thousand miles of either Scarborough or Barbados.

Two large Bar B Q ranges had been lent, courtesy of Scarborough TEC, one fuelled by butane gas, the other charcoal-fuelled. Jamie made sure there was ample supplies of both fuels as there would be nothing more untimely than to run out of one, or even both. Wasn't "dual fuel" the name of the game these days? It would be awfully embarrassing to say to a guest poised with a plate and salad: 'I'm sorry, madam, the gas has just run out. Would you like your minute steak to be thirty seconds or finished off with a charcoal flavour?' Jamie thought he might just do that one day for a laugh. Samantha Lyon was arriving with two students just after two and he was keen to introduce her to his Mum. She had heard all about her from Jamie's numerous little chat's on the phone. She and her sister, their Aunty Gwen, arrived on the train into Scarborough on time. That alone was a miracle given the almost routine "engineering works" which seemed to affect almost every track in the country at weekends. They had declined an offer of being met at the station, preferring to take a taxi to minimise the disruption to the family. They asked the driver to take the "scenic route" right around the Marine Drive, something Mandy had not done since the time they had arrived in Scarborough. It seemed a lifetime ago.

To minimise any potential embarrassment or awkwardness between them, Pete had decided to be warm but diplomatic, especially in front of the children, not that they were children any-more. He embraced them both in the drive as soon as they got out of the taxi.

'Welcome back Mandy. Just treat the place as your own.'

He was right there. She'd paid for the bulk of the bricks and mortar.

'Oh Sebbie, come here baby!'

He rose onto his hind legs and licked her hands until he was sure that there was not a molecule of salt left on her skin. A perfunctory sniff of Gwen's smart new M & S shoes and he was gone. The Ritsons had just arrived with their doggies and turned immediately into the garden with its myriad of new scents and trails. Seb followed them and a pleasurable afternoon of mutual bum-sniffing was guaranteed and, with luck, a sausage or two from the butane fuelled range. He wasn't too keen on the "cave-man" charcoal cuisine. He would wait patiently and chance his luck.

Millie took great care in making sure that all the guests were introduced to each other and was delighted that her Mum and Samantha were chatting like old friends. She hoped her Mum had remembered to bring the gift for Jamie that would put the seal of approval on his future career. She knew nothing about the special gift for Lucy that the taxi-driver had put straight into the shed to hide it from prying eyes. After all she might not live here any-more but she did remember the layout. Out of the blue, Samantha Lyon started tapping a knife so hard on the side of a champagne flute that any harder and the fragile stem might have snapped off to the ground. Clearly, she's had a glass or three of Prosecco already.

'Order please everybody, order. Thank you.' Everyone was hushed.

'Today is a special day not just because it's Jamie's and Lucy's birthdays but because it also marks a special day for Jamie.'

What was all this? She reached for a cardboard tube on an adjacent trestle table laden with salads of every description. Snapping off the white plastic top with an audible 'pop' she shook out a rolled certificate and unfurled it as if it was a Dead Sea Scroll.

'This is to Certify that James Peter Fishburn has successfully completed the elementary course in Catering and is hereby invited to enrol on the course leading to our Chef's Diploma starting …'

She didn't finish speaking. Everybody clapped and cheered and clinked their glasses with Jamie's. He was overjoyed. He'd been waiting on tenterhooks for days for the result and hadn't expected it today of all days. Samantha hadn't quite finished.'

'I'd now like to hand you over to Jamie's mum, Mandy, who would like to say a few words. Mandy.'

'Hello everyone. I'm Mandy. I can't tell you how proud I am of my son today. What a wonderful young man he's turned out to be. I could not possibly approve more of his chosen career path and to help him down this road I want to give him this gift which I hope he will treasure all his life and will hold him in good stead for ever. Thank you. Come here, love and give your Mam a kiss. He opened the beautiful navy blue box with a lid as deep as the box itself. Inside was a set of French-made Sebatier chef's knives that Egon Ronay himself would have been proud to own. Jamie blushed but did as he was told for once and gave her a smacker on both cheeks. But his Mam hadn't quite finished.

'I haven't done yet. Where's that lovely little daughter of mine – not so little now eh? Sweet sixteen, peaches and cream! Lucy, where are you, love?'

She was only seconds away and had been retrieving Seb from becoming over-familiar with the Ritson's Yorkshire terriers and seemingly willing to share a huge Cumberland sausage only with Candy from the trio of pooches from next door. Millie had been detailed to retrieve a large flat package from the shed. What was it, a picture maybe? Perhaps a remembrance of her childhood in Hull? Lucy carefully undid the wrapping. Despite its size it wasn't heavy. All was soon revealed. It was a large photo of Sebbie mounted on a canvas bloc. Sat on the beach at the North Bay with his tongue hanging out and his red ID glinting in the Scarbados sun. This boy was every inch a Cruft's Winner – even if his pedigree was of dubious distinction. Lucy burst into tears and threw both arms around her mother.

'Oh, Mam, it's beautiful. I couldn't have asked for anything better. Love you.'

Prosecco flowed like Scalby Beck in flood and the range of desserts that Samantha had organised from the college was a portent of menus and skills still to be exhibited. Mandy and Gwen both had two helpings of crème brûlée and Mandy perhaps a glass more of Chardonnay than she would normally have had. Jamie's additional information that it was a 2022 Wolf Blass from the southern Barossa Valley with hints of stone-fruits and a gravel minerality fell on deaf ears. She was far too far gone by then, in fact almost tipsy.

The pre-booked taxi arrived at spot on five o'clock for the Hull train due to depart at five-thirty. There were fond hugs and kisses on the drive from all the family and even Mandy and Pete managed a hug and an air-kiss to please the crowd. Everybody waved to everyone else. What a wonderful afternoon it had been. Not a hint of bad feeling had been in the air, none. The ladies chatted in the back seat en-route to the station.

'I say, Gwen, I think I met everybody did you? But who was that awful brassy tart, you know that one with the posh London voice? Who did she think she was – the Queen of bloody Sheba?'

'Are you sure you want to know, love? Lucy eventually told me after she's had a little sherry.'

'Go on, I'm all ears.'

'She's Pete's new squeeze.'

'You what?!'

'Yeah, his knock-off. She's stayed the weekend.'

47.

Blissfully unaware that he had been "reported to the headmistress" by his youngest daughter, Peter thoroughly enjoyed the remainder of the weekend in the company of his new beau. He hadn't felt like this for many, many years, in fact since he and Mandy had been "courting" in the old-fashioned way long before on-line dating had ever been heard of. Not that he and Pamela had met on a dating website but it had to be acknowledged that, but for the internet and the Google search for a hotel in Barbados, they would never have crossed paths let alone become physically attracted.

The drinks during the intermission at the Theatre in the Round had been their first real chance to be alone from the rest of the family. Pamela was absolutely enchanted with the theatre itself and found it almost beyond comprehension that a seaside town famous for beaches, bingo and knickerbocker glories could be the home of such a centre of culture. She was bowled over and not just by the venue. For the first time in years she had met a man from a completely different background to her own. The previous strings of men in her life had been affluent professionals in law, banking and the City. To her they had all had one thing in common – they were boring. Consequently, much to the consternation of her upper middle-class parents, she had turned down numerous proposals from would-be suitors. They had passed away, without grandchildren, in the Surrey commuter belt several years earlier. The last eggs in the carton had gone, as the late Victoria Wood once said, and she now felt free to find love without the brain-numbing responsibilities of parenthood.

This man, Peter Fishburn, was a new experience for her. A man from 'Ull who talked about a different life, one that was such a contrast to her own. She could just picture him now, in his starched P & O uniform attending to the whims and wishes of five hundred passengers at a time.

'Another beer, Sir? Have you tried the new Trappist ales we have selected recently from Flanders?'

'As an alternative to the house Merlot, Madam, may I suggest the Gold medal-winning Lobo e Falcão from Portugal. We have a new supplier in Crombé Wines from Kortrijk and it's not red, white or rosé any more.'

No wonder Peter was keen to see young Jamie doing so well. Knowledge of wines would follow a knowledge of food as sure as night follows day. It was only a mater of time. By the end of the twenty minute intermission she was totally smitten. So was he.

By the time the taxi had borne them back to the Hotel Barbados it had been late and only a brief but tender kiss on the lips had been snatched before retiring to bed – separate beds.

The next day with Mandy safely back in Hull, Pamela started to relax and was slightly more obvious in her affectation towards Peter. She was deliberately chatty to all three of his kids, especially Lucy as the youngest. She didn't know that Lucy had inadvertently spilled the beans to her Aunty Gwen the previous afternoon. Perhaps that cuddle and squeeze behind the Eucalyptus tree had been a tad too indiscreet and that Seb had not been the only witness.

Peter took Pamela to the railway station late on the Monday morning but not until after a brief dash to show her the river at Scalby Mills with its foot-bridge across to a scenic walk on higher ground. The tide was seemingly out half-way to Jutland and a myriad of sea birds pecked and strutted their way across the green covered rocks. It was now or never and halfway across the bridge she looked him straight in the eye and said:

'Peter, thank you for an amazing weekend. I just love your family and I adore your dog. Can I … can I come visit you again?'

It was just as well the answer was 'of course' because, as she had admitted in her Review, she had already cancelled her holiday in Barbados. Her journey back to London King's Cross via York was a dream but not of the next working day at the office, publishing deadlines and the hullaballoo of the frantic world of journalism. She didn't just cancel Barbados. She cancelled the intended trip to Hastings too. If her wishes and hopes came true then Miss Pamela Hesketh was going to be the next Mrs Fishburn.

48.

Peter had no sooner walked through the door after taking Pamela to the railway station when Millie shouted after him.

'Dad where have you been?! Don't you answer your mobile any more?'

'I left it on charge. It was as flat as a pancake. Why what's up?'

'Clive's been on the phone. When you didn't answer your mobile he called the hotel number. Can you call him back fairly quickly he said. And I suspect you might have had something else on your mind.' Her lips curled into a little smile at that last bit.

'I don't know what you mean young lady. So he didn't give you any clue?'

'No, he didn't. Look, for goodness sake, go into the conservatory, it's deserted. I'll bring you a coffee OK?'

Peter retrieved his by now fully charged mobile, disappeared into their little oasis and pressed the speed-dial for Clive White. Clive had seemingly become indispensable to their corporate endeavours but it was as yet minimal compared to the role he would fulfil in the months, indeed years, ahead.

'Morning Clive, or is it afternoon? The last few days have been a blur. What can I do you for?'

'Mmmmm, well I can't imagine why, unless of course your new friend had something to do with it?'

'Ha! Shush! The less said about that the better at the moment but she is a charmer isn't she? And did you see that Review in her magazine. Money couldn't buy that sort of publicity, could it?'

'You're right Peter, but remember there's always a price to pay. No such thing as a free lunch eh? Anyway, my friend, firstly, I wanted to thank you all for a wonderful afternoon yesterday. Great food, great drink and great company. And you and Mandy managed a degree of civility that was admirable in the circumstances, I thought.' Like Peter, he knew nothing of the exchange in the taxi between Mandy and her sister Gwen.

'Anyway, Peter, did you hear the News on most Radio stations this morning, you know, about the hotels, refugees etc.'

''Er no actually. My mind was on other things ...'

'I'll bet! OK so listen up. You know all this business about the public's disquiet about prominent hotels being used for housing refugees?'

'Of course, who hasn't for goodness sake?'

''Well it seems like it's all coming to an end. All those hotels, mostly in seaside towns like Scarborough, Brid and the like, are all to be returned to their normal use.'

'So how does that possibly affect us?'

'Because, my friend, one of them is not a million miles from you – The Clifftop Hotel. Do you know it?'

'No I can't say I do, why?'

'It's on the Governments disposal list. It was compulsorily purchased by the Home Office at the start of the crisis. Now they want to sell it. It's been discreetly offered through selected Agents to potentially interested parties.'

'And, so what?'

'No takers. Not even a sniff.'

'How big is it?'

'Fifty letting rooms, I believe. Three lounges and two separate dining rooms and a Bar licensed for non-residents. Oh yes, and a small ballroom cum function room. In its day it was quite posh.'

'How do you know this?'

'Because the Bank used to organise Scarborough Weekends there in May every year before the hotel got really busy. It was always over-subscribed. The highlight of the weekend was a Gala Dinner on the Saturday night – lots of inter-Branch hanky-panky I can tell you. Those were the days.'

'Sounds great but that's big, too big, way beyond our price range surely?'

'There's the rub. We don't know that. As you know I wanted to talk with you about this in general before the party but you were all too busy arranging garden furniture and your mind was obviously elsewhere.... anyway where was I?'

'There's the rub ...'

'Oh yes, the Home Office is under pressure to end the whole sorry business. The Clifftop Hotel is going to be sold by informal tender in two weeks time. Sealed bids. You've seen it on TV. Some of them are fixed of course but this one won't be.'

'So what do you think it might go for? A million and a half?

'Let's meet for lunch on Friday shall we? I'll have a think about it. How long have I told you that you need a bigger hotel?'

He hung up and walked back into the reception hall. Millie looked up and smiled a wider smile than earlier. Had Clive already apprised her of his thoughts? She was, after all, his star student and protégé. She walked round from behind the desk and pecked him on both cheeks in rapid succession.

'Go for it, Dad, just go for it. And I don't just mean the business.'

She had not seen her father look so happy for a long, long time. With all that was going on she completely forgot to tell him that the High Commissioner for Barbados and his wife would be arriving on Friday for a weekend's visit.

49.

The letter from Mandy's solicitors in Hull would normally have caused Peter extreme distress. Not now. He had a spring in his step and a new zest for life and the future. And he still had no idea what Pamela was thinking. The gist of the solicitor's letter was that Mandy wanted a divorce as expeditiously and as amicably as possible. She didn't want the childrens' future to be jeopardised in any way but she did require a fair financial settlement. It was, after all, her money that had paid for the purchase of the Wendover Hotel, now renamed Hotel Scarbados. There was also the added bonus of the newly discovered cache of Euros, now converted into Sterling and placed in a term deposit with the Blackbird Bank plc. It would all have to be taken into account. He would of course play with a straight bat even if the two overseas cricketers hadn't stayed with them, not this season at least.

Did he, should he, appoint a local firm of solicitors to act in his interests? Maybe he should consult with Clive first, and who knows, he might be able to reach an agreed settlement somehow. Events, however, were to overtake everybody within the next few days.

Friday afternoon saw the arrival of His Excellency Malcolm Morgan, the High Commissioner, and his wife Marlene. There were no diplomatic trappings of the kind that might have been laid on if they had been attending say a Dinner or Reception at the Foreighn and Commonwealth

Office in London, or a cocktail party at another Embassy or High Commission. There was no Diplomatic protection and no plain clothed security staff. Like Mandy and Gwen days earlier, they arrived in a white Station Taxi but this time a version of 'people carrier' which was just as well as considering the volume of luggage they had with them – two cases each plus small hand-held bags. Mrs Morgan's multi-coloured dress and matching flowery hat caught the ever-vigilant Seb totally off-guard. Why any human would want to resemble a herbaceous border was totally beyond him. Her husband was a different kettle of fish and he instantly sniffed and made pals with the suited West Indian gentleman. Millie was on desk duty.

'Good afternoon, your Excellency and Mrs Morgan. Welcome to the Hotel Scarbados. How was your journey?'

'Just fine thank you.' They both smiled.

'And can I say what a nice frontage your hotel has. So many palm trees!'

''Well you wait until you've seen the dining room and conservatory as we …'

'Oh yes, we saw them in the magazine feature, Didn't we Malcolm, honey?'

'You've seen that magazine? I can't imagine it being in the ante-room of your office as reading material for important people waiting for an audience.'

'Ha ha! Well nor can I really to be honest – the Reader's Digest more likely – like a dentist's waiting room! A member of our staff who was looking for a hotel to stay in while visiting relatives in Yorkshire saw the article and lent us the magazine. It is just like it in real life. Even the clock on the wall on Barbados time. I'm impressed.'

Plainly these two had a sense of humour. What a shame they hadn't been there the previous weekend to socialise at the party, thought Millie.

'Now, do we have to sign in?'

'Yes please, your Excellency, just here and here …'

'Please, it's Malcolm and Marlene while we're here OK? It's so good to get away from the nightmare of London. I'll just put H.E. in the Register if you don't mind. There we are. Now, I'll carry our bags upstairs and the room number is? Six eh? My lucky number. I always tried to hit every ball for six – in my younger days of course. What's on the dinner menu tonight? A Jamie's special?'

His Excellency hadn't just read the magazine and the special feature, he'd positively digested it.

Just after the house Gâteaux and before the coffees, Jamie came out from the kitchen still in his whites and introduced himself.

'Er, how do you do your Excellency, er …'

'Now, young man, didn't your sister tell you that it's Malcolm and Marlene? I was just about to say my compliments to the chef when I've just realised it's you! That roast pork was wonderful. Now, we have two guests joining us for dinner tomorrow night. They're unfortunately staying at another hotel just down the road as your establishment is fully booked. Now, can you do your special roast beef with Yorkshire puddings for us all as a separate starter as you say?'

'I'm sure we can do that for you. With the richest caramelised red onion gravy of course?'

'And freshly made home-grown horseradish sauce … ha ha! I read the egg sandwich description!'

'When in Rome, Malcolm, when in Rome.'

'You mean Scarbados, Jamie! Just one final question.'

'Sure, how can I help?'

'Where is the cricket ground from here? I'd like to take a good look tomorrow. Is it far to walk? I love to stretch my legs after breakfast – something that's not easy to do in

London. At least not if you don't want to get run over by a double-decker bus.'

'I'll walk with you if you like. It's about fifteen minutes, not too far.'

'That's a deal, Jamie, that's a deal.'

Shortly after eleven the next morning Malcolm and Jamie set off, taking Seb with them as a change from his normal "walkies" towards the beach. Walking up North Marine Road and turning into the narrow entrance the huge iron gates in front of them were open on one side. They walked through just as the sun came out which had hitherto failed to appear that morning. The massive green oval appeared before them like a freshly cut emerald.

'This is Scarborough Cricket Club? Wow! It's bigger than Bridgetown. I'm impressed beyond words. How much is it to join?'

'I don't know. You can get life membership for a few hundred pounds I think. You'd have to ask Mr Carter the Treasurer. Ask Dad, he can put you in touch. He often comes to the hotel. By the way if you don't mind my asking, who are these two extra folks who are coming to dinner tonight?'

'Strictly between you and I, Jamie, they're finance and treasury people over here from Barbados. It costs a fortune to accommodate and entertain people in London and I'm constantly getting my knuckles wrapped for exceeding budgets. It would be cheaper to amuse them somewhere like here and you know what the one thing Barbadians like more than sunshine and rum punches don't you?'

'Let me guess – cricket!'

"You've got it in one. Now, show me some more of this nice little town. Which way back to the sea?'

They walked straight past the Clifftop Hotel which, so far, Jamie had never even heard of. It looked deserted. Seb paused for a few sniffs as they passed by the front door. Not bad, not bad at all, he thought to himself.

50.

The two other gentlemen from the Barbados Government arrived on foot late in the afternoon and took 'afternoon tea' in the garden with the Morgans. Old habits die hard in the British Empire. It was just a shame that the cricket season had finished as it roughly coincided with the Tea interval had Scarborough Cricket Club being playing a home game that day. They would have to wait until next year. They were almost forensic in their examination of the hotel and its grounds. Something was afoot. There was more to this than met the eye. In fact a lot more. The dinner went down well and the Yorkshire puddings starter was a revelation to the two newcomers. They invited Peter to join them for coffee in the conservatory. The Morgans had gone out for an evening stroll in Peasholm Park and with the nights drawing in, dusk had fallen. A thousand fairy lights were the only illumination for this most enchanting of sylvan settings. They just hoped that the discussions back at the hotel were going well.

'Mr Fishburn, we act with the full authority of the Government of Barbados. In fact I am the Financial Secretary. In a nutshell, Mr Fishburn, my Government wishes to purchase your hotel – how do you say it here – lock stock and barrel? A formal offer will be made to you overnight and should arrive here tomorrow. I do hope you find my Government's offer acceptable.'

Peter was stunned rigid. He needed to speak with Clive White but perhaps he should wait and see what the morning brought. He didn't sleep much. Sometime during the night while he was dreaming of serving beers and wines on the mv Pride of Bruges an email landed in the inbox of the Hotel Scarbados. It was from a firm of lawyers in Bridgetown.

We act on behalf of our clients, the Government of the Republic of Barbados. Our clients wish to purchase the freehold of the Hotel Scarbados, the goodwill of the business and any associated intellectual property such as the website and other social media identities. The sum being offered is £1.2m Sterling completion to be by 1ˢᵗ December this year. Please be kind enough to confirm your acceptance to our London offices within seven days – details below.'

By ten o'clock Peter was in deep conversation with Clive White.

'Right, put them on hold. Tell them you need the full seven days to consider their offer as the family must all be consulted.'

'By that you mean Mandy, I take it?'

'Well, her solicitors in Hull, primarily. Organise a zoom meeting as soon as possible, today if you can.'

'Why the rush?'

'Because, my friend, those tenders for the Clifftop Hotel must be lodged by tomorrow. This is the plan.' It was a one-sided conversation for two minutes.

'Got it? Agreed?'

'Yes, but what if either her or her lawyers don't like the idea?'

'They will, trust me. Now, sit down with Millie and Jamie who are both legally adults now and tell them what the plan is. Just do it and get back to me.'

It was an audacious plan but by the Grace of God and a following wind, it might just come off. Within twenty four hours a new limited company had been purchased off the shelf with a totally forgettable name. It mattered not. The subscribing shareholders were Peter, Mandy, Millie and James Fishburn in equal proportion. Clive White was listed as the Company Secretary. A sealed tender offer of one million pounds was lodged for the acquisition of the Clifftop Hotel. The successful tender was announced the following morning and was reported live on the ten o'clock news bulletin on BBC Radio York.

'The Home Office has just announced that at long last one of Scarborough's best know landmarks, the Clifftop Hotel, has been sold to a local family. Further details will be released later but it puts an end to a sad and long-running saga.'

'Clive, how did you know our tender would be successful? And how did you know that Mandy's lawyers would agree to the deal?'

'Look, firstly the Home Office wanted rid of it, virtually at any cost. It's worth a lot more than that but they had to accept your offer.'

'How come?'

'It was the only offer.'

'What?! How do you know?'

'Peter, in this world it's who you know, not what you know. And as for your future ex-wife, well she's getting twenty-five percent of the shares in a hotel with huge potential, sole ownership of the former marital home back in Hull and fifty grand in cash, being a quarter of the net proceeds after the sale of Hotel Scarbados. Everybody wins. All you have to do now is open a new limited company account at the bank and then organise the date for the first Extraordinary General Meeting.'

'To do what?'

'To appoint the Directors, the Auditors and oh yes, decide upon the change of name of the company. Have you decided on the new name of the hotel yet?'

Yes we have. We've decided unanimously to call it: HOTEL KOALA.

* * *

EPILOGUE

It was a cool but sunny autumn day in the beautiful medieval City of Bruges, or Brugge, if your linguistic leanings were towards Dutch. How many folks realised that Zeebrugge simply meant 'Bruges by the Sea?'

The coast of Flanders was to Belgium what Yorkshire was to England – a summer playground. Bruges, Ostend and Blankenburg were once again flourishing after the ravages of Covid had taken their toll. Normality of a sorts had returned, for most but not all.

For Stephanie van Gelder, life would never be quite the same again. Her dear brother had passed away during the pandemic and his restaurant in Ostend, the Fleur de Lys, was now permanently closed. The ferries didn't run any more from Zeebrugge to Hull and the hundreds of previously familiar faces were no longer to be seen in the shops, cafés and restaurants of the city that compared itself to medieval York in historical splendour. Things would never be the same again.

She had seen the magazine *'English Hotels Monthy'* left behind by an English tourist in the café where she worked part-time. Upon reading the feature on the Hotel Scarbados she did a double take on the photo of the reception desk and the barometer mounted on the wall with the clocks. She knew it was the barometer she had given to Peter. Those were her initials SVG engraved in the brass. Her eyes filled with tears. Her little girl, Natalie, aged eight, gazed up to meet her mother's eyes.

'Don't cry, Mama, don't cry.'

'One day I want to tell you about your father. You've got his eyes too. Did I ever tell you that?'

First published in Great Britain by Michael Joseph Ltd
27 Wrights Lane, Kensington, London W8 5TZ

© Dulcie Gray 1987

British Library Cataloguing in Publication Data

Gray, Dulcie
    Mirror Image.
    I. Title
    823'.914 [F]   PR6013.R364

    ISBN 0-7181-2581-9

0718 125 819 2102

Typeset by Alacrity Phototypesetters,
Banwell Castle, Weston-super-Mare
Printed and bound in Great Britain by
Billing & Sons, Worcester

Mirror Image

Dulcie Gray

Michael Joseph
LONDON